A Devotional Written During COVID-19 to Encourage You Through Any Challenging Season

Hope in the Midst: A Devotional Written During COVID-19 to Encourage You Through Any Challenging Season
Copyright © 2020

Published by JVMI Publishing, a division of Jewish Voice Ministries International
P.O. Box 31998
Phoenix, Arizona 85046-1998
Phone: 800-299-9374
www.jewishvoice.org

Unless otherwise indicated, Scripture is taken from the Tree of Life (TLV) Translation of the Bible. Copyright © 2015 by Tree of Life Bible Society. All rights reserved.

Scripture quotations marked NIV are taken from the Holy Bible, New International Version®, NIV®. Copyright © 1973, 1978, 1984, 2011 by Biblica, Inc.™ Used by permission of Zondervan. All rights reserved worldwide. www.zondervan.com The "NIV" and "New International Version" are trademarks registered in the United States Patent and Trademark Office by Biblica, Inc.™

Scripture quotations marked NKJV are taken from the New King James Version®. Copyright © 1982 by Thomas Nelson. Used by permission. All rights reserved.

Scriptures quotations marked NASB are from the New American Standard Bible, Copyright © 1960, 1962, 1963, 1968, 1971, 1972, 1973, 1975, 1977, 1995 by the Lockman Foundation. Used by permission. www.Lockman.com

Printed in China

Unauthorized duplication is prohibited. To purchase copies of this publication or for permission to use, please contact Jewish Voice Ministries International by phone or via the web as listed above.

ISBN 978-0-9993391-4-5

Table of Contents

Introduction 5

Hope from Jeremiah 9
Day 1: Taking Hold of Hope During Darkest Times 10
Day 2: God's Unchanging Character 13
Day 3: Living, Healing Waters 16
Day 4: Curing the Incurable Disease 19
Day 5: Our God is Faithful 22
Day 6: Extravagant Hope 25
Day 7: Hope, Even in Prison 29

Hope from Exodus 33
Day 1: Hope in Knowing He Hears Our Cry 34
Day 2: Hope in the God Who Guides 36
Day 3: Hope Through the Blood of the Lamb 39
Day 4: Hope When Idols Fail 42
Day 5: Hope in the God Who Provides Me with Rest 45
Day 6: Hope in God's Purposes Even in Hard Times 48
Day 7: Hope Through Pursuing the God Who Draws Near . . . 51

Hope from Revelation 55
Day 1: He is our Hope and Overcomer 56
Day 2: Find Hope and Overcome Through Praise
and Proclamation 59
Day 3: Overcoming by the Blood of the Lamb
and the Word of our Testimony 62
Day 4: Finding Hope and Overcoming Through Worship 65
Day 5: We have been Invited to the Wedding Banquet
of the Lamb 68
Day 6: Hope and Encouragement Found in the Tree of Life . . . 72
Day 7: The Spirit and Bride Say Come! 75

Hope from James 79
Day 1: Pure Joy in the Midst of Trials 80
Day 2: Draw Near to God in This Season 82
Day 3: Gain Access to the Lord's Wisdom 84
Day 4: Speaking Life in Difficult Times. .86
Day 5: How to Have Community while Social Distancing. 89
Day 6: The Lord's Will in This Season 92
Day 7: Perseverance in Trials 95

Hope from Philippians 97
Day 1: From the Beginning until Completion 98
Day 2: The Advancement of the Kingdom 100
Day 3: Rejoicing Through Every Circumstance. 103
Day 4: The Lord's Great and Unfailing Love. 106
Day 5: Experiencing the Shalom of God. 108
Day 6: Abiding in Yeshua 110
Day 7: Cultivating Encouragement in our Communities. 112

Hope from Isaiah 115
Day 1: More Than Bread 116
Day 2: Purified for Purpose 118
Day 3: Beyond Roadblocks 121
Day 4: Holy Boldness. 123
Day 5: A Stump of Hope 126
Day 6: Covenant Family 129
Day 7: Rest & Living Water 132

Hope from Romans 135
Day 1: Hoping Against All Reason. 136
Day 2: From Trouble to Hope. 138
Day 3: Hope Does Not Disappoint 142
Day 4: Waiting with Eager Hope 145
Day 5: A Stronger Hope. 148
Day 6: Hope and Comfort in the Scriptures. 151
Day 7: Filled with Hope and Joy. 153

Hope from Ephesians **157**
Day 1: Hope in His Calling. 158
Day 2: We are His Workmanship. 160
Day 3: Fill Me Up Please 162
Day 4: My Words Matter. 164
Day 5: A New Day 166
Day 6: Get Dressed, Even If You Have Nowhere to Go. 168
Day 7: Encouragement and Hope 170

Hope from Ezra-Nehemiah **173**
Day 1: In Three-Part Harmony. 174
Day 2: The Stirring Begins 178
Day 3: In the Midst of Opposition. 183
Day 4: Shavuot, A Musical Interlude. 188
Day 5: A Renewed Covenant 192
Day 6: A Prepared Heart. 196
Day 7: Future Glory. 199

Introduction

In the spring of 2020, a highly contagious coronavirus upended the world with fear, stay-at-home mandates, financial loss and isolation. For nine weeks during that time, Jewish Voice Ministries International published daily blog posts containing scriptural messages of hope to help Believers through the rough times. The world opened back up slowly after the global pandemic. People emerged to resume life, perhaps somewhat timidly, wondering how we would fare as things work their way back to "normal" – whatever that will look like now.

Soon after things began opening up in America, racial tensions peaked, and social distancing mandates fell prey to mass protests. New levels of widespread instability landed on our doorsteps.

One thing we know: We still need God's hope – every day. So, it seemed natural to compile these insights and encouragement into a book that can be revisited. *Hope in the Midst* is a collection of nine separate devotional series, each seven days long and authored by various Jewish Voice staff members during a particularly hard time in the world. Each one is focused on a different book of the Bible. It is a snapshot of a period in history when most of the entire world stayed home in isolation, vastly altering our lifestyles as we tried to stop the spread of a global pandemic.

At the same time, this book is a resource to find hope in the midst of any trial you may face. God's Word is timeless. In it, we find the spiritual resources to help us throughout our life journeys. Though these devotions were written during the initial COVID-19 lockdowns of 2020, their messages remain relevant for any season in which we find ourselves in need of hope.

Each author brings their own devotional approach, with unique writing styles and different presentations. However, through these varied voices and Scriptures, we see some common themes emerge. God encouraged us to find hope amid trials by:

- Giving thanks, being grateful, and searching for joy
- Remembering our great salvation and the sacrifice of Yeshua (Jesus) for us
- Praising and worshiping God
- Fixing our eyes on Jesus and dwelling on the good
- Looking to the ultimate fulfillment of our hope – the great future that awaits us in heaven
- Lifting our eyes off ourselves and reaching out to serve others – by praying for others, extending grace and searching for ways to encourage and bless others.

Each one of these brings hope and joy into our experience. They lift our spirits and refocus our hearts on the good that is all around us, even in the midst of suffering, hardship or periods of tedious, uncertain waiting.

Here's a brief overview of some of the strength-giving, hope-inducing truths you'll find on the following pages.

Hope from the book of Jeremiah

From Jeremiah, we see that even when everything seems dark, asleep or dead, God is attentive and ready to accomplish His promises. We learn that we can cling to God's unchanging character even amid drastically changed circumstances. We find hope in the reassurance that God can and will visit us in our personal "prisons," be they our homes, anxieties, loss or our awareness that we've been living far from Him.

Hope from the book of Exodus

Through Exodus, we learn that we can rest in the fact that even when we feel lost, God knows the way, and He offers guidance through difficult times. We take hope that, though we are susceptible to placing our hope in false things, God is faithful and continues to reveal Himself as worthy of our trust and hope.

We see that living with an intentional awareness of His presence brings us joy, hope and peace.

Hope from the book of Revelation
We find Revelation filled with hope for both our heavenly future and today. We see that we need not fear because Jesus is our hope and encouragement, and He has already overcome. We overcome by His finished work on our behalf and proclaiming what He's done in our lives. We experience victory and lifted spirits when we worship God and hope when we fix our eyes on the fulness of Heaven awaiting us.

Hope from the book of James
James invites us to see trials and hardships as opportunities to grow closer to God. We are reminded that wisdom is ours for the asking and that patiently enduring trials produces blessing. We see how a challenging time can show us what is essential and to let those things push aside the nonessentials of life. We are encouraged to look for joy.

Hope from the book of Philippians
From Philippians, we learn that abiding in Messiah empowers us to experience the life-giving fruits of His Spirit in all situations. We see that no circumstance can remove us from God's love and, in clinging to it, it is powerful enough to sustain us amid suffering. We find peace and joy in casting our concerns on God and dwelling on His good gifts, and we can rejoice that God uses even the most difficult times to advance His Good News.

Hope from the book of Isaiah
Looking at the book of Isaiah, we see that though God's timetable for resolving our trials may be different than ours, He is trustworthy. God promises to provide for us, guide and strengthen us. He uses the fires of purification to remove worthless things from our lives to make room for the good He wants to bring. God invites us to rest in Him, recognizing that our deepest needs can only be satisfied in Him.

Hope from the book of Romans
Romans teaches us that God is a God of hope, able to fill us with all joy and peace as we believe and trust Him. Through Romans, we see that God's hope sustains our faith by grace and despite our circumstances. We discover that we can choose hope over despair because we serve a promise-keeping God. We learn that hope is even stronger when it is braided together with joy, patience and prayer.

Hope from the book of Ephesians
Ephesians reveals that God's deep love for us is the same amid difficulty as it is during ease. We see that His will is for us to rejoice, pray and give thanks. We are encouraged to clothe ourselves now with the Word and His spiritual armor in preparation for when unsuspected battles for our peace or focus come. We see that our worth is grounded in Jesus, who is the awesome, powerful ruler of all things.

Hope from the books of Ezra and Nehemiah
These books show that God has hope for us today, the near future and eternity. The strength of our hope rests in God's faithfulness, and even in seasons of waiting, we can live with expectant hope for the good future He is even now working to produce. We are reminded that opposition will come, but as we build our lives on God, seek His Word and use the tools He's given us, we rest on an unshakeable Rock.

Taking hope with us every day
These truths are not just for times of world crisis. They will help us get through personal crises, both major and minor. The hope we encountered over the weeks and months during the coronavirus lockdown is hope that we can – and need to – carry with us into each day.

The Scripture is full of God's hope, joy and peace. Stay in it. Go to it often, searching for Him and His goodness. As you do, you will discover deeper layers of His trustworthiness, His love and His power to see you through all things with joy. May you carry His unshakeable hope with you in the midst of each and every day.

"Nevertheless, I will bring health and healing to it; I will heal my people and will let them enjoy abundant peace and security."

—Jeremiah 33:1-3,6 NIV

Week 1

HOPE
FROM JEREMIAH

Ezra Benjamin
Vice President of Global Ministry Affairs

Day 1
Taking Hold of Hope During Darkest Times

The word of the Lord came to me: "What do you see, Jeremiah?"
"I see the branch of an almond tree," I replied. The Lord said
to me, "You have seen correctly, for I am watching
to see that my word is fulfilled."
—Jeremiah 1:11–12 NIV

The prophet Jeremiah bore the heavy burden of delivering messages from Heaven to the kings, priests, and people of Israel about the pending judgment for their sin, the destruction of Jerusalem for her idolatry, and coming captivity of the Jewish people into foreign lands. Despite the difficulty of his role and the darkness of the season he would have to walk through with his fellow Jewish people, Jeremiah would have found comfort in knowing from the beginning of his ministry that God had hand-picked him for this task even before he was formed in his mother's womb (Jeremiah 1:5).

God knew Jeremiah from before he existed and set him apart for his unique prophetic ministry. Time and again, He came to Jeremiah at critical moments to remind him that – even when difficulty abounded, when his message was ill-received, and when despair loomed all around – his destiny and calling were secure because the heart and the promises of God were sure.

In the first chapter of Jeremiah, only a few verses after understanding that he had been brought into existence for the purposes of delivering God's messages to Israel and to the nations, the Lord shows Jeremiah the blossom on an almond tree. Through this blossom, God confirms that the words He has spoken and the promises He has made shall surely come to pass. For the Lord is 'watching over' or 'intently hastening' to accomplish them.

Interestingly, the almond tree (*shakéd'* in Hebrew), was one of the first trees in Israel to put forth its blossoms at the end of winter. The tree was likely named based on the root Hebrew word – which means "hastening" or "on the watch" – to be the first to spring into action. While all other trees were sleeping, and before any others sprouted their leaves, the *shakéd* would spring into bloom around January. Still late winter! But it was a sign that other things were about to awaken, that spring – a new season – was on its way.

The Lord affirms Jeremiah's observation of the *shakéd*, and says, "…for I am watching over (*shoked*) My word to perform it." The same root Hebrew word! In this case, God was assuring Jeremiah that He is "hastening" or keeping watch to seize the first opportunity to accomplish what He has promised. Jeremiah understood, and we can join our confidence with his, that God, like the almond tree is ready to spring into action FIRST to speedily accomplish His promises, even when everything else around seems to be dark, asleep, or even dead.

Jeremiah did not see all of what God spoke through him come to pass in his lifetime, but he did see most – because God hastened to accomplish it according to His promise. God has made many promises to us – in His word, and to us personally in our lives. And in this season, as we have seen fear, uncertainty, darkness, and even a "shadow of death" spring up so quickly around the world, we can and must fix our hope on the reality that – even more than the trouble around us – God's word, His promises, are waiting and hastening to spring into action, un-delayed and undiluted by the trouble and slumber around us. By His grace, and in full assurance of faith, let's guard against falling asleep or succumbing to the winter of dread or despair. Let's remain alert and full of hope, watching for the promises of God to come quickly to life in this season – for God is hastening to see that they do! Spring is here! May His promises spring to life in us and through us as we wait expectantly upon Him.

Thoughts, Reflections and Prayers:

Day 2
God's Unchanging Character

This is what the Lord says: "Let not the wise boast of their wisdom or the strong boast of their strength or the rich boast of their riches, but let the one who boasts boast about this: that they have the understanding to know me, that I am the Lord, who exercises kindness, justice and righteousness on earth, for in these I delight," declares the Lord.
—Jeremiah 9:23–24 NIV

The coronavirus pandemic has, if nothing else, revealed to us the fragility of life. It has challenged the things we held as unchangeable, unbreakable and impenetrable. And it has caused us to re-evaluate our priorities in light of the newly underscored reality that anything can change – and it can change in an instant. All the wisdom of man and medical expertise is, as of yet, unable to come up with a cure or even a speedy treatment. The wealth of great men and nations has not prevented economies from grinding to a halt in only a matter of days. And powerful men, like even the Prime Minister of the United Kingdom, have shown themselves just as susceptible to this illness as the humble factory worker living in a hut somewhere in the Chinese mountains.

Jeremiah faced a similar situation. The Lord would judge the kings and people of Israel because they had forsaken Him, rejected dependence on their Maker and had considered themselves immune to sudden disaster. They trusted in their intellect, military strength, wealth, religious systems and leaders rather than casting themselves on the One who had always promised to carry them, protect them, and be with them in trouble. Through Jeremiah, God reminds Israel (and us!) that no amount of boasting or dependence upon our modern science and understanding, our bank account and investment balances or our personal or national strength and power will insulate us in a day of real trouble.

God exhorts Israel (and us!) to look again. To reevaluate her priorities. To take stock of her situation. To consider carefully what systems or assets she has placed her trust in up until this point. And to come to the good, right, and life-saving conclusion that the best, wisest, most powerful, and most valuable treasure and refuge we could possess in this world – even the one about which we should glory and boast openly – is our knowledge and understanding of God Most High. To understand His unchanging nature, trust in His promises, and depend upon His goodness even – especially – in times of trouble.

Did God "cause" coronavirus? No! We do not serve a God who creates evil. Is God "allowing" coronavirus? Certainly. Why? To punish mankind? To teach the nations a lesson? To bring the world to the point of desperation such that they cry out to Him? To demonstrate His healing power? The truth is, we don't know. But God tells us that what we can know. The most valuable knowledge and understanding we can carry with us in this season of uncertainty is that the Lord will always "exercise lovingkindness [mercy], judgment [perfect judgment] and righteousness in the earth." For this is His glory. This is who He is (Jeremiah 9:23).

Let's take a hold of the invitation in Jeremiah during this unprecedented season – where man's wisdom, power and riches are being tested and found wanting – to press in to, and even boast with joy and confidence in, the knowledge of the unchanging character of God. May His character (compassionate and gracious God, slow to anger and abounding in lovingkindness…longsuffering, not willing that any should perish but that all should come to salvation and eternal life) fill us with hope, and may our knowledge of that character through faith and by His Spirit fill us with great joy and gratitude (Exodus 34:6, 2 Peter 3:9). For these things can never be taken away.

Thoughts, Reflections and Prayers:

Day 3
Living, Healing Waters

Lord, you are the hope of Israel; all who forsake you will be put to shame. Those who turn away from you will be written in the dust because they have forsaken the Lord, the spring of living water. Heal me, Lord, and I will be healed; save me and I will be saved, for you are the one I praise.
—Jeremiah 17:13–14 NIV

As we watch COVID-19-related death tolls rise day by day, and as we grapple with the fragility of life, Jeremiah's words here should both challenge and comfort us. God is indeed the HOPE of Israel, since His lovingkindness is everlasting, and He is always good.

The concept here of being "written in the earth" literally means "written in the dust" – the idea being that the wind would blow, the writing would disappear, and the memory of what had been written would vanish away. God warns Israel that those who abandon Him to serve other gods, or to serve themselves, shall not be remembered. Their lives, like writing in the dirt, shall vanish away.

Amid the uncertainty, business closures, shelter-in-place orders and myriad of other restrictions throwing off our well-established routines, most of us have found ourselves queuing up outside grocery stores and wholesale markets or shopping incessantly online. Storing up food and supplies, buying what we need to survive in case we find ourselves suddenly in survival mode. We have scurried around our towns grabbing what we can, always asking, "How many weeks until I run out? Could I make it on this much? Do I have what I/my family needs to make it to the end of this disaster? Or do I need more?" We think so, but we're just not sure… And we wrestle with the questions, "How much is enough?" and "What if I run out?"

Yeshua, revealing in Himself the same character and provisions of God as revealed in this passage in Jeremiah, cuts right to the heart of the matter in John 4:13–14. The Samaritan woman, despised by many around her for her ethnic identity, had to risk the trip to the well in the heat of the day, after all others had taken their share. And she would have to come back, blistering day after blistering day. Jesus reminds her that the water she was drinking would indeed never be enough. She would thirst again. But if she would turn to Him, rivers (fountains) of living waters would flow from within her. She would not only have enough, she would have more than enough, and waters would flow out of her life into the lives of those around her. God exhorts Israel to not turn away from Him to things which can never satisfy, only to find their names erased in the fragility of life. He exhorts them to return to Him, the fountain of living waters, and have their names written in the Book of Life, which shall never be erased though Heaven and Earth should pass away.

Jeremiah, though chosen by God and full of faith, recognized that he too had – at times and in part – forsaken those living waters with which the Lord wanted to fill and satisfy him. He too, like each of us, though committed to the Lord, was a sinful man with the incurable wound of a fallen nature and the need for a touch from Heaven. But in the face of this stark realization in a time of crisis, Jeremiah makes an amazing declaration of faith. Not "Heal me that I may be healed" or "Heal me, that I might be healed." But, "Heal me, and I *shall* be healed."

Like Jeremiah, we can know and find hope in the fact that – though life is fragile, though the conveniences of life may run out, and though we struggle with sin and brokenness felt all the more acutely during crisis – we serve a God who, through faith in His Son Yeshua, is filling us today with overflowing rivers of life and who, if we ask Him, can and will heal us from all our diseases. We shall be healed! Hallelujah!

Thoughts, Reflections and Prayers:

Day 4
Curing the Incurable Disease

"I am with you and will save you," declares the Lord. "Though I completely destroy all the nations among which I scatter you, I will not completely destroy you. I will discipline you but only in due measure; I will not let you go entirely unpunished." This is what the Lord says: "Your wound is incurable, your injury beyond healing. There is no one to plead your cause, no remedy for your sore, no healing for you.... But I will restore you to health and heal your wounds," declares the Lord, "because you are called an outcast, Zion for whom no one cares."
—Jeremiah 30:11–13, 17 NIV

Right now, perhaps the most unsettling fact (and one which should drive all Believers to a place of greater dependence upon God alone) is that, as of yet, there is no remedy for coronavirus. No cure, no vaccine, no simple treatment which reduces symptoms or complications. The pervasiveness of the pandemic and the lack of any surefire way to dodge sickness has us feeling – to whatever degree – vulnerable, anxious, and hesitant to accept the reality that we need answers we just do not have.

In this passage of Jeremiah, we encounter both the kindness and the severity of God. We, as did Israel, find confidence in the nearness of God who is mighty to save, mighty to restore, mighty to regather. He is mighty to bring about divine justice on His enemies and those who had persecuted His people in their time of distress. He is faithful to care as a trustworthy Shepherd for those whom He has called His own.

But God brings Israel face-to-face with a harsh reality: Even in the midst of the promises, in the midst of their election, in the midst of God's nearness, they are incurably ill. They have a disease with no remedy and there is no one who can help. Those who courted Israel in the good times are nowhere to be found. She now sits alone, wounded, ill, with no earthly hope of recovering. The Father makes it abundantly clear in this passage that this incurable disease – this seemingly fatal wound – has come upon Israel because of the desperate state of her own sinfulness.

This time of great uncertainty we're going through, this shaking of the nations, and the physical presence of an as-of-yet unpreventable disease, can leave us, like Israel, feeling helpless and even despairing. But, in the providence of God, who works all things together for good for those who press into Him in love (Romans 8:28), this can be an opportunity to reflect with truth AND hope on a deeper reality.

The truth is, I have an incurable disease. And, so do you. And, so does everyone around you. It is the sinful nature of my flesh. It is the reality that, in myself, there is no righteousness. The diagnosis that, on my own and apart from God's intervention, I would have been left to die from the pandemic of sin. We are all subject to this incurable illness for which there is a 100% death rate.

But the HOPE is that there is One who can, and desires to, restore "health" to Israel and to me. To heal all my wounds and free me from this disease. God was able to offer help, hope and a cure for Israel's incurable disease because He is mighty to save and because He knew that He would offer a perfect Lamb – His Son Yeshua – whose blood would be the balm and whose own wounds would bring healing and relief from the incurable disease of sin that results in death.

We believe that God, in His mercy and longsuffering, can and will intervene in the coronavirus pandemic. And we pray daily to that end. May we also remember though, that we can believe this *because* of the larger cure He has already brought forth: the cure for sin and death – for Israel if she will receive it, and for you and for me. While we don't yet see the cure or the end of this physical pandemic, we can take hope and rest assured that we have the cure – by His grace through faith – for the greater disease for which there was no other cure. And we can share this cure, this hope, this confidence, this relief, this transformative message, with friends, family, and coworkers as they ask the deeper questions during this time. Take hope!

Thoughts, Reflections and Prayers:

Day 5
Our God is Faithful

"The days are coming," declares the Lord, "when I will make a new covenant with the people of Israel and with the people of Judah. It will not be like the covenant I made with their ancestors when I took them by the hand to lead them out of Egypt, because they broke My covenant, though I was a husband to them," declares the Lord. "This is the covenant I will make with the people of Israel after that time," declares the Lord. "I will put My law in their minds and write it on their hearts. I will be their God, and they will be My people.... This is what the Lord says, "He who appoints the sun to shine by day, who decrees the moon and stars to shine by night, who stirs up the sea so that its waves roar—the Lord Almighty is His name: "Only if these decrees vanish from My sight," declares the Lord, "will Israel ever cease being a nation before Me."
—Jeremiah 31:31–33, 35–36 NIV

In times like these, we are forced to re-evaluate what is certain. Things we have taken for granted have suddenly been called into question. *Will there be food on the shelves when I go shopping? Will I have a job three months from now? I eat healthy and exercise...but can I be sure I won't get sick? And if I do, will I receive the care I need? When will I see my family member or loved one again – the one I put off visiting in the busyness of life? Will the government, or my pastor for that matter, really be able to help me if things get tough?*

Questions without answers bring us to a crossroads where we either switch to self-preservation and survival mode, or we ask the scary question: After all, and no matter what, what is it in my life that I can depend on beyond any circumstance? What in my life is secure, regardless of how my life may look at the other end of this trial?

Amid the dark and difficult message Jeremiah delivers to the inhabitants of Jerusalem regarding their impending calamity and exile because of their sin, a bright streak of hope emerges. God told Israel He would do something new. Though she had broken the covenant made at Sinai over and over again, and though her disease – her propensity to sin – was incurable (Jeremiah 30), God was making another way.

The broken covenant could not be put back together. Israel's wound was incurable, but God would heal her to the uttermost by doing a new thing, making a new covenant. It would be a better covenant in the sense that while the requirements of the first were impossible to meet because of the incurable depravity of the human heart in its fallen condition, the new covenant would actually be written upon our minds and hearts. It would be a covenant not made by the blood of bulls and goats, but one made once and for all in the blood of the Passover Lamb, the Great High Priest, Yeshua the Messiah. And that new and better way would be open not only to Israel, but also to all who would receive it by faith. So, Israel's hope and confidence were not in her own faithfulness, but in the faithfulness of God to keep His promises to His people and to make a way where there had been no way.

But how could Israel be sure God would preserve her as a nation? Disaster loomed on the horizon. The death of many was inevitable, and through Jeremiah, they had come face to face with a deep, heartbreaking awareness of their own wicked ways. Could this new and living way that was to come really be certain? Could they count on it? Could they proclaim it and share it with their neighbors? Can we also depend upon God's promises when the systems and structures around us cease to be dependable? God's declaration in Jeremiah 31:35–36 holds the answer: As surely as the coming of the dawn, and as surely as the moon and stars are in the sky at night, that's how certain His commitment to preserve and sanctify His people is. No matter how dark the night, every dawn reminds us of His great faithfulness. No matter how disastrous the day, every evening sky appears as a renewed promise that He will preserve those who call upon His name.

Hope in the Midst

How can we be certain of God's faithfulness in these difficult times? Simple! Because Israel still exists as a people today. The very existence of the Jewish people is a banner to the nations and a promise to all of us who call upon His name that He is the faithful promise keeper.

How do we know that God remains enthroned in Heaven, that He remains good in the midst of hardship and intimately committed to care for us and preserve us for eternity with Him? Because the sun rose this morning. How do we know He will keep the promises He has made to us though the world around us groans and shifts? Because the moon and the stars will come out tonight. During these difficult times, may we rejoice in the One who has drawn Israel and all of us near to Him through a new and living way in Yeshua. May each morning and each evening renew our HOPE that every promise He has made will come to pass.

Thoughts, Reflections and Prayers:

Day 6
Extravagant Hope

Jeremiah said, "The word of the Lord came to me: Hanamel son of Shallum your uncle is going to come to you and say, 'Buy my field at Anathoth, because as nearest relative it is your right and duty to buy it.'

"Then, just as the Lord had said, my cousin Hanamel came to me in the courtyard of the guard and said, 'Buy my field at Anathoth in the territory of Benjamin. Since it is your right to redeem it and possess it, buy it for yourself.'

"I knew that this was the word of the Lord; so I bought the field at Anathoth from my cousin Hanamel and weighed out for him seventeen shekels of silver. I signed and sealed the deed, had it witnessed, and weighed out the silver on the scales. I took the deed of purchase—the sealed copy containing the terms and conditions, as well as the unsealed copy— and I gave this deed to Baruch son of Neriah, the son of Mahseiah, in the presence of my cousin Hanamel and of the witnesses who had signed the deed and of all the Jews sitting in the courtyard of the guard.

"In their presence I gave Baruch these instructions: 'This is what the Lord Almighty, the God of Israel, says: Take these documents, both the sealed and unsealed copies of the deed of purchase, and put them in a clay jar so they will last a long time. For this is what the Lord Almighty, the God of Israel, says: Houses, fields and vineyards will again be bought in this land.'

... And though the city will be given into the hands of the Babylonians, you, Sovereign Lord, say to me, 'Buy the field with silver and have the transaction witnessed.'"

"Then the word of the Lord came to Jeremiah: "I am the Lord, the God of all mankind. Is anything too hard for me?"
—Jeremiah 32:6–15, 25–27 NIV

May this passage of Scripture and these words inspire your hearts to "dream big" during a time when the thinking of those around us may be very narrow.

This portion of Jeremiah's prophetic ministry occurred when he was imprisoned and the city of Jerusalem around him was being ravaged by the Babylonian armies, just as the Lord had warned. Houses were being burned, families were being murdered or carried away captive, and the outlook was only disaster and loss. No doubt, the thoughts of the Israelites around Jeremiah were focused on survival and, at best, minimizing the human and financial loss they would experience due to the unrelenting disaster which had come upon their city and nation. And for good reason! All the indicators said this was the time to hunker down and stay alive.

Sound familiar?

Yet, in the middle of this grim scene, the Lord asks Jeremiah to make an extravagant investment. And to do so in a formal and public way in the audience of his companions who were focused only on survival. Not only that, Jeremiah was to document the extravagant investment in such a way that it would be remembered in later generations. God told Jeremiah to purchase a plot of land – at a time when land was being urgently sold, if not violently destroyed – as a prophetic declaration that the promises of God to rebuild and restore would surely come to pass despite the immediate disaster.

The humanity of Jeremiah in this passage should bring us comfort. Jeremiah, knowing that the entire real estate transaction is from the Lord, still cries out to Him for understanding. *Such a large investment during such dark times? Lord, I am obeying what You told me to do, but why now, in the midst of this crisis?* God answers Jeremiah's question with another, and far more important, question: *I am the God of all flesh – the Creator of every person on the face of the earth – whether they acknowledge it or not. Is there anything too hard for Me?* (Jeremiah 32:27).

The answer to Jeremiah's doubts regarding the radical obedience and sacrificial investment God called him to in the midst of societal disaster was the nature and power of God Himself. And the answer was, of course, a resounding "No." Nothing is too hard for the Lord. The Lord proceeded to confirm to Jeremiah what he already saw around him – that death and loss would certainly visit the city and the people – but that the Lord, the God of all flesh, would turn the situation around for good for His people. Better days were on their way! Days when a people, humble and repentant, would remain and would return, and that which was lost would be restored.

Jeremiah's public real estate transaction was a radical declaration to those around him of his *hope* that nothing was too difficult for His God. They illustrated that where others could see only to the horizon of loss and chaos, Jeremiah could see days ahead with heavenly promises fulfilled, days of revival and restoration.

At a time when the counsel of this world is largely (and understandably) to hunker down and survive the dark times, what extravagant act of hope and faith might God be asking you to make? To what counter-intuitive, counter-cultural act of faith-filled obedience is God calling you? What investment – financial, relational or time (perhaps in an estranged or lonely family member) – is God asking us to make? Kingdom investments which will demonstrate to those around us that we fully believe this is not the end, that God has promises yet to fulfill, that He is *able* to restore what has been lost, and that there are dreams the Father has placed in your heart for His glory which have yet to be realized. Let's pray for strength and grace in the waiting, for faith for radical obedience in the most difficult of times. And let's rest in *hope* today because there is nothing too difficult for our God.

Thoughts, Reflections and Prayers:

Day 7
Hope, Even in Prison

While Jeremiah was still confined in the courtyard of the guard, the word of the Lord came to him a second time: "This is what the Lord says, he who made the earth, the Lord who formed it and established it—the Lord is his name: 'Call to me and I will answer you and tell you great and unsearchable things you do not know.' ... "Nevertheless, I will bring health and healing to it; I will heal my people and will let them enjoy abundant peace and security."
—Jeremiah 33:1–3,6 NIV

Today we are filled with awe that the God who delivered the Israelites from the plague of death through the blood of lambs, and the One who pronounced that all men (Jew and Gentile alike) are separated from Him by sin, would send the great Passover Lamb – the Lamb of God, Yeshua Himself who takes away the sins of the world – to suffer and die for us. And we rejoice that He did not stay in the grave, but rather conquered it! Today, we remember the Jewish men and women who, recognizing Jesus for who He truly was, laid their palm fronds on the streets leading to the Temple gates and cried out *"Hoshiana!"* – Hosanna, meaning, literally "Save now, Lord!"

But the emotions and awe of the week ahead may be tempered – even squelched – by the reality that most of the world will spend it, as well as the entire month, at home, stuck inside, isolating, protecting ourselves and our families from illness, and waiting to see what will happen. Many of us may feel anxious, irritated, even trapped. Many are frustrated with constant contact with spouse and children; others who live by themselves are facing the stark reality of spending these community-oriented holidays alone. Our worlds, once full of busyness and freedom, have suddenly become very small. How do we engage the Lord from the individual "prisons" of a quarantined world?

Jeremiah, due to the severity and unpalatability of the Lord's word through him, also found himself imprisoned against his will. The situation throughout Jerusalem was already grim. Armies were attacking, people were perishing, and hope was scarce. Yet, though Jeremiah could not venture out, the word of the Lord came to him. "Call to Me, and I will answer you, and show you great and mighty things" (Jeremiah 33:3 KJV). The word *great* here, means high and wonderful things. *Mighty*, in Hebrew, means things which had been full of secret and mystery, things previously unattainable – even more than that – things actually fortified and made inaccessible.

God meets Jeremiah in his prison with a simple invitation. Just call to Me. Just inquire of Me. Just ask Me. It's a simple invitation with a glorious, life-changing, ministry-shaping result: that God would answer from Heaven and reveal to Jeremiah wonderful things which had actually been made inaccessible and kept secret prior to this moment. Things which Jeremiah, a prophet of God with years of experience serving the Lord and speaking forth His words, still did not know.

In a sense, God was saying, "I'll open to you things and wisdom which have been locked away and kept back because you have not asked Me." What Jeremiah had not known, what he had lost sight of in the midst of the turmoil and imprisonment, is that though the Lord had allowed such darkness and destruction, His sure promise was to bring "health and healing" to the city and its people. And not just physical healing, but that, out of the ashes would come a revelation of the abundance of peace [shalom] and truth" (Jeremiah 33:6).

On this Palm Sunday, at the beginning of this Passover Week and in the midst of coronavirus, God can and will come to us and visit us in the prisons we are in – whether that's our homes, anxieties, lack, or perhaps a keen awareness that we have been apart from Him and aren't sure how to get back. God invites us afresh to call to Him. To inquire of Him as to both the reality and the *hope* of our situation. And He promises that, as surely as the coming of the dawn, He will answer our cries by showing us great and wonderful things – things kept back until we asked – things we haven't yet known. Things which will strengthen and enable us to walk, filled with hope, through this difficult time. Because we know that health, healing, and the abundance of shalom and truth, are on their way. Hoshianah!

Thoughts, Reflections and Prayers:

"My presence will go with you, and I will give you rest," He answered.

—Exodus 33:14

Week 2

HOPE
FROM EXODUS

Paula Walberer
Prayer Program Supervisor

Day 1
Hope in Knowing He Hears Our Cry

...I have heard their cry...
—Exodus 3:7

There's a popular worship song that is encouraging so many of us with reminders that God is the One who makes a way as He works miracles and keeps His promises. One of my favorite lines in the song underscores that this is happening even when I am not aware of it.

The song could have been written as an encouragement to the children of Israel in captivity. They were crying out to the Lord for deliverance, even when they had no evidence that He was hearing them in the very hardest of times. Still, they kept faith, even though they couldn't see that He was preparing to deliver them and preparing His human instrument, Moses, whom He would use to do it.

The Lord was listening and ready to move on their behalf in response to their cries. What an attentive and gracious Deliverer! He is attentive to your cries too.

Where in the Word: Exodus 3:7–10

Finding Hope
PONDER: What do I read about God in this passage that gives me hope?

PRAY: How can this recharge my prayers as I call on the God who hears the cries of His people?

RESPOND: Moses had to act in ways that were outside his expectations and comfort zone. How might God be calling me to participate in what He is doing in my life and world? Include prayers and acts of service for others who are crying out at this time.

Something more to think about with God: Romans 8:24–27

Day 2
Hope in the God Who Guides

You in Your lovingkindness led the people You have redeemed. You guided them in Your strength to Your holy habitation.
—Exodus 15:13

When I was a little girl, we took a cross-country trip from Arizona to New England. My dad brought a big United States atlas and used a yellow highlighter to mark our route from state to state to state, all the way to my cousin's hometown in Massachusetts. I loved tracing my finger along the route, even though all the different place names, roads, and symbols were confusing. I was also very aware that I had never been to these places before. However, my father knew the way – we ended up at my cousin's house and eventually returned safely back home.

In Exodus, we see our Heavenly Father's attentive care and guidance for His children as He led them on their cross-country journey through the wilderness. They truly were in uncharted territory, and it must have been daunting. They didn't have a map with highlights, but instead, God gave them supernatural direction through the cloud by day and the pillar of fire by night. He even tailormade the route just for them.

As Creator, God had expert knowledge of the terrain, the dangers and circumstances, and the human frailty of possible responses of His people. Now, He offers guidance for us, His children – guidance for today and all the way home.

Where in the Word: Exodus 13:17–22

Finding Hope
PONDER: How are you sensing the Lord's guidance, both in this story from Exodus and in your own unfolding story right now?

PRAY: Put your thoughts and concerns about the pathway ahead of you into prayer. Ask God, your Father, to show you the way.

RESPOND: When the Children of Israel saw the pillar of fire or the cloud move, they had to respond and move too – or be left behind. Other times they just needed to stay put. Is there some guidance or direction the Lord is giving you that you need to act on?

Something more to think about with God: Isaiah 42:16

Day 3
Hope Through the Blood of the Lamb

…And when I see the blood I will pass over you…
—Exodus 12:13 NIV

I love celebrating Passover each year. When I was a teenager, the biblical account of the Passover became meaningful in a way that touches me to this day. The Lord used that story shared in a simple Gospel pamphlet to help me understand the gift of salvation through Yeshua. It was about how the Children of Israel, by faith, applied the blood of a spotless lamb on their doorposts and lintels, and once that had been done, the people inside that home were safe.

I had been struggling with fear that I wouldn't be able to believe big enough to truly be saved, but this little booklet helped me see that it wasn't about what I could accomplish. What had already been done through the blood is what mattered and made the difference. Through faith in what Jesus, the Lamb of God, accomplished through the shedding of His blood, I was safe – and saved!

The Passover story is one of the most meaningful in Scripture. It reflects back to the Garden of Eden and the need for Adam and Eve to be covered by the skins of animals that were killed. It reminds us of Abraham not having to sacrifice Isaac because God provided a ram. It tells us about God's deliverance of His children from cruelty and slavery. And it points forward to the ultimate remedy and provision for sin and death through the sacrifice and resurrection of our Savior, Deliverer and Messiah, Yeshua.

Doesn't that fill you with gratitude and hope? Doesn't that make you want to *tell somebody*?

Where in the Word: Exodus 12:1–16

Finding Hope

PONDER: Where do you imagine yourself in the story of the Passover? Would you be confident or fearful? Why? Where do you see yourself in the story of the Good News?

PRAY: If you have not received God's gift of salvation through Jesus' sacrifice, talk with God about that now! If you have received Him, pray for someone else who needs to know this Good News.

RESPOND: Is the Lord asking you to share with someone the amazing Passover story and the gift of salvation to which it points? Who? Ask God for an opportunity, and take it.

Something more to talk about with God, family and friends:
Exodus 12:46, Isaiah 53, John 19:33–37, John 1:29

Day 4
Hope When Idols Fail

"I am the Lord your God, who brought you out of Egypt, out of the land of slavery. You shall have no other gods before me."
—Exodus 20:2–3 NIV

How did the Children of Israel find themselves in flagrant sin and under God's weighty wrath in the second half of Exodus 32? No doubt by way of a long slippery slope. Their propensity for idolatry is revealed in numerous passages, including the simple things mentioned in Exodus 16:3 (meat, bread, Egypt). By the time we get to the story of the golden calf, their hope was no longer in God.

They forgot the Faithful One who delivered them from Pharaoh and parted the Red Sea so they could pass through safely on dry ground. Instead they asked for new gods (the former gods of Egypt) to lead them. The idols they decided to worship would only lead them to death.

Even after His righteous judgment for their sin, God went on to show the Israelites mercy. He gave Moses a fresh promise that His presence would go with them. And in chapter 34, He gave a revelation of His character and holiness that, to this day, is regarded as sacred by Jewish people around the world ("The Thirteen Attributes" of God in Exodus 34:6–8).

We too are susceptible to idolatry, placing our hope in that which is false instead of in Him who is true. Yet the Lord, in His faithfulness, continues to reveal Himself to us as worthy of our praise, worship and hope. He will never fail.

Where in the Word: Exodus 32:1–8, 31–35, 33:14, 34:6–8

Finding Hope
PONDER: How are your current circumstances revealing false idols in which you may be finding comfort or placing your hope?

PRAY: God's kindness leads us to repentance, and honest confession and repentance bring renewed awareness of His forgiveness. Talk things over with Him now.

RESPONSE: Spend some time in God's presence, renewing your hope in Him through worship. Write out your worship to God.

Something more to talk over with God: Colossians 1:12–20

Day 5
Hope in God Who Provides Me with Rest

"My presence will go with you, and I will give you rest," He answered.
—Exodus 33:14

When the children of Israel were slaves of Pharaoh, there was no rest. However, the Lord graciously brought His people into the practice of Shabbat, and even prioritized it as one of the Ten Words (Ten Commandments). It was a day of sabbath rest to remind them He, as Creator of the world, rested after His work.

Because He delivered them and provided for them, they were now able to trust and honor Him with their day off. It was to be a special sign between them and Adonai that they were dependent on Him, set apart for Him, and could rest in Him.

The sacred rhythm of Shabbat calls across the centuries, inviting us to remember and honor our Creator and look forward to the full realization of the Messianic kingdom. Observing a time of rest and restoration each week is an act of faith, an admittance that our own efforts will never be enough. Shabbat is a weekly re-set that reorients our perspective and reminds us He is the center of our stories and the source of our hope.

Where in the Word: Exodus 16:29–30, 20:8–11

Finding Hope
PONDER: What is draining you in this season? Take time to journal and process. Do you have a weekly rhythm of rest that honors God as Creator and enables you to experience renewal?

PRAY: Spend some time with God, not asking, not telling, but just being with Him and enjoying Him. What might this time reveal to you about rest and about your need for it?

RESPOND: From a place of trust and gratitude, block out a weekly "date" with God to enjoy spending time with Him in fellowship and re-creation.

A TIMELY NOTE: In this present season, what are you doing if you have extra time on your hands? How can you be sure that some of that time is intentionally invested in your relationship with God, so you can experience rest and renewal and not just distraction?

Some more to talk with God about: Mark 6:31, 2:27, Matthew 11:28

Day 6
Hope in God's Purposes Even in Hard Times

So ADONAI said to him, "What is that in your hand?"
"A staff," he said.
—Exodus 4:2

Shiphra and Puah were Hebrew midwives who defied a cruel and powerful despot out of fear of God and to avoid a genocide of Hebrew babies. Bezalel and Oholiab were skilled craftsmen called out of their usual work into leadership and execution of God's blueprint for the Tabernacle. And Moses was drawn out of the water and into the palace, then banished to the desert and later raised up to lead the people of God.

Exodus 4:2 and the subsequent accounts of miracles show how God started with Moses right where he was and with what he had, a staff. Exodus tells amazing accounts of ordinary people, in their everyday lives, being singled out for the purposes of God.

Each of these individuals and others suffered hardships and obstacles in order to live out their God-given destiny for His glory and the benefit of others. We may not be convicted to take on a risk as dangerous as the two brave midwives, a project as immense as the Tabernacle, or a stewardship as vast as that of Moses. But we too are called to God's purposes during hard times and challenging assignments.

The same God who protected baby Moses, invited mortals to prepare a dwelling place for His presence and led His people through dreary days and awe-inspiring miracles has made you for His purposes today. The way that we listen, respond moment by moment, lay aside our own agendas and place our hope in Him is what will determine our partnership with Him and His purposes, both in this time and over our lifetime.

Where in the Word: Exodus 1:15–21, 31:1–6, 4:1–5

Finding Hope

PONDER: Moses was called to the desert for 40 years to herd sheep, which turned out to be excellent preparation for leading God's people through the wilderness. How may God be using the things in your life right now to develop your character and calling? Be specific, and thank Him.

PRAY: Acknowledge and offer to the Lord any questions, discouragement or uncertainty you may have about where you are in your life circumstances right now. Allow Him to renew your hope in Him and the things you can't yet see.

RESPOND: Read the three Scripture accounts above. Which do you relate to most? Journal how the Lord might be asking you to respond in your own life.

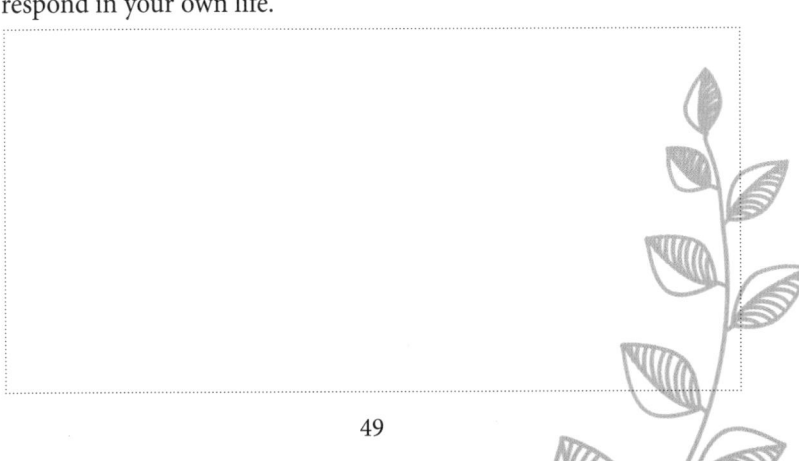

Something more to talk about with God: Philippians 2:1–18

Day 7
Hope Through Pursuing the God Who Draws Near

"Have them make a Sanctuary for Me,
so that I may dwell among them."
—Exodus 25:8

From the garden of Eden to the New Jerusalem, the Lord shows us over and over how much He desires to make Himself known to us and dwell or be with us. Consider His appearing to Moses in the burning bush, the revealing of His attributes and righteousness on Mount Sinai, and the detailed construction of the Tabernacle which foreshadowed Jesus' life on Earth among us. These are some of the examples in Exodus of God's pursuit of His people through presenting Himself, giving revelation of Himself, and making ways for His people to encounter Him.

Moses understood the importance of living in ongoing awareness of God's presence. He pressed into knowing God intimately and wouldn't risk the well-being of himself or the children of Israel by making a move apart from Him. God pursued Moses, and Moses pursued God.

Moses met with the Lord daily to worship, ask for guidance and pray for the people and issues he had been given stewardship over. He knew he couldn't go it alone, and he was faithful to seek God and His presence in prayer.

As Believers in Jesus, we now have God's presence indwelling us personally. He could not be any nearer! What a miracle! What an amazing relationship to appreciate and cultivate.

Where in the Word: Exodus 33:13–18, 34:5–8

Finding Hope
PONDER: God's instructions for building the Tabernacle are specific and detailed. How attentive might He be to the building of

His relationship with you? And how do things look from your end? What are some of the ways you are purposefully pursuing Him?

PRAY: Ask the Lord to fill you with awe and wonder at His pursuit of you and His indwelling Spirit within you.

RESPOND: Do a simple study on the Tabernacle, especially the way the structure and furnishings speak about Jesus and our relationship with God. How might this awareness move from your head to your heart?

Some more to talk to God about: John 14:1–3, Ephesians 3:17, Revelation 21:3

The One giving testimony to these things says, "Yes! I am coming soon!" Amen!
Come, Lord Yeshua!

—Revelation 22:16-20

Week 3

HOPE
FROM REVELATION

Lee Weeks
Associate Director of Congregation
& Leadership Development

Day 1
He is our Hope and Overcomer

The revelation of Yeshua the Messiah, which God gave Him to show to His servants the things that must soon take place.
—Revelation 1:1

Jesus declares that He is our hope and has overcome. In Revelation chapter 1, we find that God is revealing and has revealed Jesus as our salvation, but He wants us to see Him as not just the suffering servant but also as the King of kings and Lord of lords. Look how John describes Jesus and how Jesus reveals Himself to John in this chapter. John says:

> *…Messiah Yeshua, the faithful witness, the firstborn of the dead, and the ruler of the kings of the Earth. To Him who loves us and has freed us from our sins by His blood and made us a kingdom, kohanim [priests] to His God and Father—to Him be glory and power forever! Amen!*
> —Revelation 1:5–6

Yeshua then reveals Himself:

> *I am the Alpha and the Omega," says ADONAI Elohim, "Who is and who was and who is to come, the Almighty!*
> —Revelation 1:8

Next, John begins to describe the revealing of the glorified Messiah:

> *I saw One like a Son of Man, clothed in a robe down to His feet, with a golden belt wrapped around His chest. His head and His hair were white like wool, white like snow, and His eyes like a flame of fire. His feet were like polished bronze refined in a furnace, and His voice*

*was like the roar of rushing waters. In His right hand
He held seven stars, and out of His mouth came forth
a sharp, two-edged sword. His face was like the sun
shining at full strength.*
—Revelation 1:13–16

John is stunned and even says that he wants to fall down like a dead man. But Jesus gives John hope, encouragement and inspiration to overcome! Look at what Jesus says:

*Do not be afraid! I am the First and the Last, and
the One who lives. I was dead, but look—I am alive
forever and ever! Moreover, I hold the keys of death
and Sheol [Hell].*
—Revelation 1:17b–18

WOW! Look at how Yeshua teaches us:

- Don't be afraid!
- I live forever!
- I hold the keys of death and Sheol!

Jesus gives us the ultimate way to find hope, encouragement, and the path to overcoming. He does this by revealing to us that He lives forever and has all authority in Heaven and on Earth. Jesus shepherds our lives and hearts by encouraging us to look at His overcoming work.

My encouragement to you is, "Don't be afraid!" We are in unchartered times in history right now, but that doesn't mean we need to be fearful or do not have a hope. Our hope is in Him. He has overcome!

I hope this dive into the beginning of Revelation has inspired and encouraged you. Take some time to carefully reflect on the questions below, and journal your answers.

What is God saying in His Word?

What is God saying to me?

How should/can I respond?

Day 2
Find Hope and Overcome Through Praise and Proclamation

Chapter four of Revelation gives us insight into the scene around God's throne. John says, "immediately he was in the *Ruach* [Spirit]," and he began to see the eternal reality of worship around God's throne. Look at what John sees:

> *The four living creatures, each having six wings, were full of eyes all around and within. They do not rest day or night, chanting,*
>
> *"Kadosh, kadosh, kadosh ADONAI Elohei-Tzva'ot, asher haya v'hoveh v'yavo! Holy, holy, holy is the Lord God of Hosts, who was and who is and who is to come!"*
>
> *And whenever the living creatures give glory and honor and thanks to the One seated on the throne, who lives forever and ever, the twenty-four elders fall down before the One seated on the throne and worship Him who lives forever and ever. And they throw their crowns down before the throne, chanting,*
>
> *"Worthy are You, our Lord and God, to receive glory and honor and power, for You created all things, and because of Your will they existed and were created!"*
> —Revelation 4:8–11

What an incredible sight! John says the angels and elders around God's throne never cease to say that He is Holy. The elders submit to His authority by casting their crowns, and then they proclaim His sovereign rule over all things. I think that we can find hope and ways to overcome difficulty in this life by following the things contained in this passage.

1. Seek things that are above, where Messiah is seated (Colossians 3:1)

2. Focus our minds on things above, not on things on the Earth (Colossians 3:2)

3. Now that our minds are focused on things above, we are ready to join with the heavenly host and *praise* and *proclaim* that He is holy and worthy

4. Finally, don't miss this key example from the elders in Heaven: they submit to God's sovereign rule over all things

If you find yourself with anxiety, fear or uncertainty during these times, then follow the example above. Let's focus our minds on Him so that we can praise Him and proclaim His holiness even in trying times.

Take some time to carefully reflect on the questions below, and journal your answers.

What is God saying in His Word?

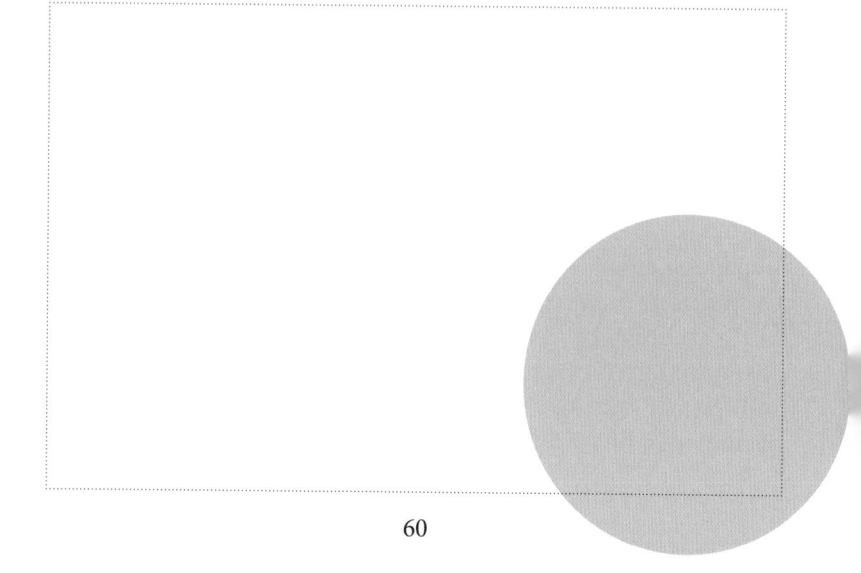

What is God saying to me?

How should/can I respond?

Day 3
Overcoming by the Blood of the Lamb and the Word of our Testimony

Then I heard a loud voice in Heaven saying, "Now have come the salvation and the power and the kingdom of our God and the authority of His Anointed One, for the accuser of our brothers and sisters—the one who accuses them before our God day and night—has been thrown out. They overcame him by the blood of the Lamb and by the word of their testimony, and they did not love their lives even in the face of death."
—Revelation 12:10–11

Chapter 12 of Revelation speaks of the "accuser of the brethren" and the "ancient serpent" or "Satan" being cast down from Heaven to the Earth. Now, the point of this devotion is not to focus on the theological timing of this event, but to draw out how to overcome the evil one.

We see in this chapter that when Believers are faced with the fury of the evil one against them, there is a way to overcome. The Scripture above says that Believers overcome the evil one "by the blood of the Lamb and the word of their testimony."

There is deep meaning to these two statements. One is based on the work of another (Yeshua) and an action. The second pertains to a declaration of our testimony to God's work in our lives.

Overcoming by the blood of the Lamb
Jesus is our perfect Passover (Pesach) Lamb. He alone has accomplished the saving work for us, yet we must apply the blood of the Lamb to the doorpost of our hearts and lives to overcome.

Overcoming by the word of our testimony
We overcome by faithful commitment to God and by declaring His goodness in our lives. We are even willing to declare that we

will not waver from our faith in Jesus during trials, tribulations or even in the face of death.

I want to encourage you to find hope in this passage. When we apply the blood of Lamb to our hearts and lives and commit to faithfully declaring God's goodness to us, then we overcome!

Take some time to carefully reflect on the questions below and journal your answers.

What is God saying in His Word?

What is God saying to me?

How should/can I respond?

Day 4
Finding Hope and Overcoming Through Worship

Here in chapter 15, we get another view into a future scene of Heaven. John says he saw another "great and wonderful sign in Heaven." This is the sign:

> *And I saw something like a sea of glass mixed with fire, and those who had overcome the beast and his image and the number of his name standing by the sea of glass, holding the harps of God. And they are singing the song of Moses the servant of God and the song of the Lamb, saying,*
>
> *"Great and wonderful are Your deeds, ADONAI Elohei-Tzva'ot [Lord God the Almighty]! Just and true are Your ways, O King of the nations! Who shall not fear and glorify Your name, O Lord? For You alone are Holy. All the nations shall come and worship before You, for Your righteous acts have been revealed!"*
> —Revelation 15:2–4

John sees another scene of worship in Heaven (note there are a lot of these in Revelation), and again he says the context of this worship scene consists of those who have overcome. There are those who overcame the beast and his image and are now standing on the sea of glass, worshiping with singing and instruments. They are singing after victory!

I hope you're beginning to see some of the pattern in the book of Revelation – that a key element of Heaven and of those who overcome difficulties on Earth both employ worship. If you find yourself struggling to overcome difficulties in your life, or wrestling to face the current situation we find ourselves in around the world, might I encourage you to use the key element of worship to lift your life and find victory. Join all of Heaven, and worship!

Take some time to carefully reflect on the questions below and journal your answers.

What is God saying in His Word?

What is God saying to me?

How should/can I respond?

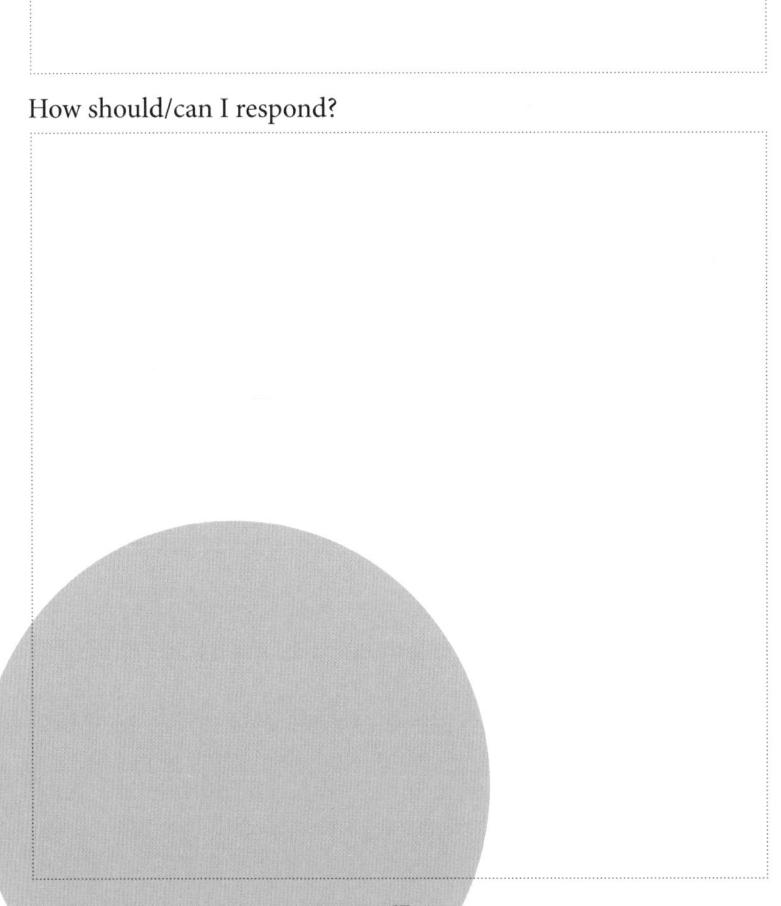

Day 5
We have been Invited to the Wedding Banquet of the Lamb

Then I heard something like the voice of a great multitude—like the roar of rushing waters or like the rumbling of powerful thunder—saying,

"Halleluyah! For Adonai Elohei-Tzva'ot [Lord God the Almighty] reigns! Let us rejoice and be glad and give the glory to Him! For the wedding of the Lamb has come, and His bride has made herself ready, she was given fine linen to wear, bright and clean! For the fine linen is the righteous deeds of the kedoshim [saints or holy ones]."

Then the angel tells me, "Write: How fortunate are those who have been invited to the wedding banquet of the Lamb!" He also tells me, "These are the true words of God."
—Revelation 19:6–9

In chapter 19 of Revelation, John writes that there is a future wedding – and not just any wedding – the wedding banquet of the Lamb. How marvelous is this new information and invitation! Or is it really new? Let's take a look in Scripture.

Jesus told a parable about the kingdom of Heaven, and He compares it to a wedding feast. He stated that a wedding banquet was being prepared; many were invited, but some were not ready. And He even says the right wedding clothes were important (Matthew 22:1–11).

Later, Jesus told another parable about wise and foolish virgins, comparing the kingdom of Heaven (or Day of the Lord) to 10 virgins waiting for the bridegroom. Yeshua states that five of the virgins were wise and five were foolish, but all grow weary in waiting for the bridegroom to appear. When he does appear, only the five wise virgins were prepared and entered the wedding feast (Matthew 25:1–12).

> *...And those who were ready went in with him to the wedding feast, and the door was shut. Now later, the other virgins came, saying, "Sir, Sir, open up for us!" But he replied, "Amen, I tell you, I do not know you." Therefore stay alert, for you know neither the day nor the hour.*
> —Matthew 25:10b–12

Now, back to the book of Revelation, where we read this portion of chapter 19 with new lenses. Jesus has given us context and some clarity about this event, but John is now seeing and giving us details into this future event at its culmination. These details should greatly encourage us:

A great multitude
John sees a great multitude! The encouragement here is that there is a great multitude of Believers throughout time who not only receive the invitation to Yeshua's wedding banquet, but are seated at the table.

Worshiping and praising
This multitude is worshiping and praising God that this day has come! This multitude were like the five wise virgins waiting for their bridegroom.

The bride has been made ready
John tells us that the "bride" (of Messiah) has been made ready and has been given the proper wedding attire to wear. John also says that the fine bright and clean linen that the guests are dressed in are the righteous deeds (*mitzvah*) of the Believers (holy ones).

You've been invited
Finally, an angel says to John "how fortunate are those who have been invited to the wedding banquet." The angel goes a step further to make sure John writes down that "these are the true words of God." This day and these words are real and true!

I hope you can find encouragement in these passages as I have over the years. Jesus has invited a multitude to His wedding day, and it will be a glorious day! What He asks of us is to be ready, living a faithful life, devoted to loving Him and others. When we do this, we are fulfilling good deeds (*mitzvah*) that make us bright and clean on His wedding day.

When trials come, our human tendency can be selfishness or operating from the flesh rather than love and the Spirit. I encourage you to picture this day when you are faced with difficult times, days, weeks and even people. When we operate from a place of hope because we have a great future, then we will live from the place of love and good deeds. Let's not be those invited who were not ready, but rather, those who overcome through hope and love.

Take some time to carefully reflect on the questions below and journal your answers.

What is God saying in His Word?

Hope from Revelation

What is God saying to me?

How should/can I respond?

Day 6
Hope and Encouragement Found in the Tree of Life

Then the angel showed me a river of the water of life—bright as crystal, flowing from the throne of God and of the Lamb down the middle of the city's street. On either side of the river was a tree of life, bearing twelve kinds of fruit, yielding its fruit each month; and the leaves of the tree were for the healing of the nations.
—Revelation 22:1–2

We have come to the last chapter in the book of Revelation, and in it, we reach the crescendo of the whole Bible, from Genesis to Revelation. Now, if you want the full context of Revelation 22, I suggest you read chapters 19–21 first and then read chapter 22. However, for this devotional I will provide a little context.

In chapter 21, we find that there is a new Heaven and a new Earth, with the addition of the New Jerusalem, coming down out of Heaven to Earth. When we move into chapter 22, we find God the Father and Jesus reigning from the New Jerusalem. This city is described in great detail, but one of the things John sees, and makes sure to point out, is the Tree of Life.

Now, this is interesting. We all know the story of Adam and Eve in the Garden and how they took the fruit from the Tree of Knowledge of Good and Evil but were removed from the Garden before they could take a bite from the Tree of Life. So, what is it about this tree and why is it so special? John gives us some insight, and I believe it will give you hope and inspiration to overcome.

John says that the Tree of Life bears fruit continually, and its leaves heal the nations. John sees this tree in the New Jerusalem, the holy city, as a source of power and healing. Now, just a few verses later, John reads some powerful words from Yeshua who uses the Tree of Life as a reward or inspiration for why we should be hopeful and overcome!

> *Then he tells me, "Do not seal up the words of the prophecy of this book, for the time is near. Let the evildoer still do evil, and the filthy still be filthy, and the righteous still do righteousness, and the holy still be holy. Behold, I am coming soon, and My reward is with Me, to pay back each one according to his deeds. I am the Alpha and the Omega, the First and the Last, the Beginning and the End. How fortunate are those who wash their robes, so that they may have the right to the Tree of Life and may enter through the gates into the city."*
> —Revelation 22:10–14

What I want to point out and focus on about the Tree of Life is that Jesus could have listed many rewards and pointed out many amazing things about the eternal age and our future rewards. However, what He highlights as a motivator and a privilege when He returns to judge is the right to the Tree of Life!

Jesus says "Behold My reward is with Me, to pay back each one according to his deeds," and the primary motivator He uses to inspire hope to do righteous acts (mitzvah) and be holy is the Tree of Life. Notice the tree is in the holy city, and you need access to get there. Jesus says if you overcome in this life, you also gain the right to "enter through the gates into the city" where the Tree of Life is located.

Maybe you have not thought about the Tree of Life in a long time, but here, Jesus reminds us of this tree that Adam and Eve lost the right to in Genesis. Now, at the end of the story in our recorded Scriptures, He says that upon His return, by overcoming in this life, we gain the right to the Tree of Life and to enter the New Jerusalem. Remember, Jesus prayed for us to be one with Him and the Father (John 17) and to be where He and the Father dwell in glory. It started in the holy garden and will end in a holy city. At the center will be the Tree of Life.

Take some time to carefully reflect on the questions below and journal your answers.

Hope in the Midst

What is God saying in His Word?

What is God saying to me?

How should/can I respond?

Day 7
The Spirit and Bride Say Come!

"I, Yeshua, have sent My angel to testify these things to you for My communities. I am the Root and the Offspring of David, the Bright and Morning Star." The Ruach [Spirit] and the bride say, "Come!" And let the one who hears say, "Come!" Let the one who is thirsty come—let the one who wishes freely take the water of life! I testify to everyone who hears the words of the prophecy of this book. If anyone adds to them, God shall add to him the plagues that are written in this book; and if anyone takes away from the words of the book of this prophecy, God shall take away his share in the Tree of Life and the Holy City, which are written in this book. The One giving testimony to these things says, "Yes! I am coming soon!" Amen! Come, Lord Yeshua!
—Revelation 22:16–20

I think this is one of the most amazing passages in Scripture, this final section in the last chapter of Revelation. Here, Yeshua not only gives us a great encouragement but also a warning. Adding to this beautiful passage is an interjection from the *Ruach* (Spirit) and the bride (body of Messiah). Let's dig in to find hope, encouragement and the inspiration to overcome.

Jesus says He sent an angel to John to testify of all the things we have seen and heard in Revelation. Then He begins to reveal and solidify His identity to all of us as the One who is the full Messianic revelation of who the prophets saw in the Torah and Tanakh (Old Covenant Scriptures). Yeshua says "I am the Root and the Offspring of David, the Bright and Morning Star."

Then, suddenly, we have an interjection from the *Ruach* and bride, who say "Come!" Those who hear, those who are thirsty, and those who wish to take the water of life are encouraged to "Come!"

Jesus ends our holy Scriptures with encouraging words testifying that He is the One declaring the prophecies of Revelation are true and that He is coming soon!

The final words of Jesus, John, the Spirit and the bride give us an anthem and a chorus to believe in, hope in and overcome with until He returns. *Bo Yeshua bo!* Come, Jesus, come!

As we end this devotional week, I encourage you to join with all the Believers from history, the great cloud of witnesses, all of Heaven, and "set your hope completely on the grace that will be brought to you at the revelation of Yeshua the Messiah" (1 Peter 1:13).

Take some time to carefully reflect on the questions below and journal your answers.

What is God saying in His Word?

What is God saying to me?

How should/can I respond?

Blessed is the one who perseveres under trial because, having stood the test, that person will receive the crown of life that the Lord has promised to those who love him.

—James 1:12 NIV

Week 4

HOPE
FROM JAMES

Carly Berna
Vice President of Marketing
and Communications

Day 1
Pure Joy in the Midst of Trials

Consider it pure joy, my brothers and sisters, whenever you face trials of many kinds, because you know that the testing of your faith produces perseverance. Let perseverance finish its work so that you may be mature and complete, not lacking anything.
—James 1:2–4 NIV

Joy and trials don't seem like words that go together very well. When I think of joy, I think of spending time with my family, hanging out with friends, and celebrating life's moments with others. Right now, most of us can't do any of these things because we are in quarantine. We are either alone or with close family, and we can't see or be around other people. It doesn't feel very joyful. It feels difficult, frustrating and confusing, among many other emotions.

The Greek word for "joy" used in this verse is *chara*, which can be translated as cheerfulness, calm, delight or gladness. These are all emotions many of us wish we had right now. But what James is exhorting is that we can take hold of these emotions because trials test our faith and produce perseverance.

As Believers, we desire to be mature in our faith. We want to show others what a strong faith is, but that strength often comes through trials. In addition, the word used here for "perseverance" can be translated to steadfastness, constancy, and endurance. I long for this in my life, and I know you do too.

A handful of years ago, I went through a pretty intense medical situation. During that season, it definitely didn't feel joyful, but looking back, the Lord was so near to me, and He never left my side. I experienced great peace and a testing of my faith like never before. It allowed me to grow in compassion, mercy, and patience, especially with others. I wouldn't have learned those lessons if it wasn't for that experience.

A change in perspective can allow us to see the current trial of the coronavirus as an opportunity to strengthen our faith. Consider it a workout for your faith. Allow yourself to build your muscle of faith through exercising your strength and patience day in and day out. Look around you to find the joy in your situation. See it as a chance to grow closer to the Lord.

As you are in quarantine, either by yourself, or with others, take stock of what is happening around you. Maybe keep a journal of the emotions you are feeling throughout the day. Find the moments of thanksgiving, and find the joy in the situation. Write down what you are thankful for. Use this to draw near to the Lord as you recognize His goodness in the midst of this trial. Use it also to encourage others around you who can't seem to see past the difficult situation.

Practical Takeaway: Record your thoughts and feelings as well as your thanksgiving and praise to the Lord!

Thoughts, Reflections and Prayers:

Day 2
Draw Near to God in This Season

Come near to God and he will come near to you…
—James 4:8 NIV

This season that we find ourselves in is very hard to comprehend. It doesn't make sense; we don't understand it, and we didn't expect it. Thankfully for us, it's not a surprise to the Lord. We can take confidence in the fact that despite our circumstances, He doesn't change, and His promises are still true. Hold to that thought when you feel discouraged.

One of His encouraging promises is in James 4:8. As we draw near to the Lord, He draws near to us. This is so comforting. God is not hidden from us during this time. In fact, He is near to us. He is our comforter, and He will never leave us. Although you may feel alone, take heart that the Lord is near. Use this time to draw near to Him in ways you never have before. I pray you experience His presence as a result.

Like many of you, I find myself having a lot of time on my hands. Now that we are in lockdown, there are not as many activities to fill our time. There is more isolation, more silence, and more time for reflection. Use this opportunity to draw near to the Lord. Think about some of the ways you used to spend your time and if it was fruitful. Are there new practices you can put in place that will help you to draw near to the Lord?

Perhaps you can re-energize your quiet time, reading your Bible or journaling. Listen to an encouraging podcast or sermon. Play worship music and fix your thoughts on Him. Pray for your family, friends and neighbors. Sit quietly, and listen for the Lord to speak to you. Take a walk, and look for God's presence in nature. Praise Him, and thank Him for all of the blessings you have.

Spiritual disciplines are an important part of our walk with the Lord, and they enable us to draw near to Him. You may have great spiritual rhythms already in place, or you may feel like you are lacking in this area. Take some time to look at your daily, weekly, monthly, or even annual spiritual rhythms, and determine if there is something you need to implement that will help you to be closer to Him. Try something new in this season! May the Lord surprise you as He draws near to you.

Practical Takeaway: Conduct an inventory of your spiritual disciplines, and draw near to the Lord in new ways.

Thoughts, Reflections and Prayers:

Day 3
Gain Access to the Lord's Wisdom

*If any of you lacks wisdom, you should ask God, who gives
generously to all without finding fault, and it will be given to you.*
—James 1:5 NIV

*But the wisdom that comes from heaven is first of all pure; then
peace-loving, considerate, submissive, full of mercy
and good fruit, impartial and sincere.*
—James 3:17 NIV

If you've ever watched a 3-D movie you know what it's like to be totally engrossed in a story. There are multiple dimensions and layers. A 2-D movie is engaging, but it is nothing compared to a 3-D movie where it feels like the characters are reaching out and touching you. When watching a 3-D movie, you even have to wear special glasses so you can understand what is going on, otherwise, it just looks blurry, foggy and doesn't make sense. This example is similar to the world's wisdom, which can seem confusing because it's not God's perspective. On the other hand, God's wisdom is beyond us, and we need to put our trust in Him and understand His good and perfect plans and purposes.

Our wisdom doesn't compare to God's wisdom. The word "wisdom" used in James is the Greek word, *sophia*, which comes from the root word, *sophos*. The meaning of this word is to form the best plans and use the best means for their execution. God brings the best results through the best means. His ways are higher than our ways.

Not only can we rest in the fact that God is executing the best results, James says that we can have access to this wisdom ourselves if we ask God. You may be facing situations right now where you desperately need wisdom. This may be a financial or relational situation; you may have a physical or medical crisis, or you may just need wisdom to understand how to proceed through the coronavirus situation without living in fear. Ask God for wisdom through these times, and He will grant you access to it.

As I mentioned, God's wisdom allows for the best results through the best means, but it also comes with other characteristics detailed in James 3:17. It's pure, peace-loving, considerate, submissive, full of mercy and good fruit, impartial and sincere. What great benefits we have access to through our heavenly Father!

I encourage you to not try to navigate this season alone. Seek the Lord's direction and wisdom. Tell Him what you're struggling with. Ask Him for wisdom and clarity. Pray to receive His wisdom.

Also, pray for others around you. Everyone needs wisdom right now: our world leaders, our fellow Believers, our neighbors, friends and family. Ask the Lord to guide us all by granting us His wisdom.

Practical Takeaway: Determine those around you who need God's wisdom, and pray for them. Look at your own situation, and identify where you need the Lord's wisdom. Then ask Him for it.

Thoughts, Reflections and Prayers:

Day 4
Speaking Life in Difficult Times

*...Everyone should be quick to listen, slow to speak
and slow to become angry.*
—James 1:19 NIV

*With the tongue we praise our Lord and Father, and with it we curse
human beings, who have been made in God's likeness. Out of the
same mouth come praise and cursing. My brothers and sisters, this
should not be. Can both fresh water and salt water flow from the
same spring? My brothers and sisters, can a fig tree bear olives, or a
grapevine bear figs? Neither can a salt spring produce fresh water.*
—James 3:9–12 NIV

*Brothers and sisters, do not slander one another. Anyone who
speaks against a brother or sister or judges them speaks against the
law and judges it. When you judge the law, you are not keeping it,
but sitting in judgment on it. There is only one Lawgiver and Judge,
the one who is able to save and destroy. But you—who are you to
judge your neighbor?*
—James 4:11–12 NIV

During this season of social/physical distancing, it's important that we are still engaging with others in a biblical way. We shouldn't let the distancing make us draw away from others. I was taking a walk recently and every time I saw a person on the sidewalk, I noticed how much I was paying attention to making sure I was six feet away from them. Thoughts crossed my mind like, *Should I cross the street? Should I walk into the dirt? Should I look away when they pass?* I used to smile and wave at people I walked by, and even say hello. I don't want this season of distancing to turn into a season of avoidance or frustration with others. While we are stressed and have heavy burdens, we should make sure we are displaying an attitude that reflects Jesus to others.

James gives us great instructions on how to use our words and actions to bless others. He gives three simple reminders: be quick to listen, slow to speak, and slow to become angry. In this season, everyone is going through something. Everyone has some kind of anxiety, something that is causing difficulty. So, it's especially important that we take the time to listen to each other. Allow yourself to be curious with your friends and family and hear how they are processing. Then, respond slowly and intentionally. Be encouraging.

In addition, it may be frustrating that others are not dealing with COVID-19 the same way you are. Maybe they live in a different state and have different lockdown requirements. Remember James' words to be slow to become angry. Take this time to be patient with others. Show Jesus' love and patience to those around you and in your life, Believers and non-believers. Pray for them, and remind them that God is still in control.

James details and reminds us of the power we have in what comes out of our mouths. It may be easy to judge and talk about others, but we shouldn't criticize or slander our neighbor. We have an incredible opportunity and the power to speak life-giving words to others in a very difficult season. Use this time to reach out to those around you – maybe send them a text or email, write them a note, or call them. Everyone could use some encouragement, and, as you are able to bless others, you will most likely be blessed as well.

I encourage you to think about those you are interacting with, whether it's your friends, family or coworkers. Take stock of how you can be a voice of encouragement in their lives. Write down their names, and determine steps for how you can reach out, listen to what they're going through, and share a Scripture or other words of affirmation that will bless them.

Practical Takeaway: Make a list of others you are interacting with and determine steps to bless them through your words.

Thoughts, Reflections and Prayers:

Day 5
How to Have Community while Social Distancing

Is anyone among you in trouble? Let them pray. Is anyone happy? Let them sing songs of praise. Is anyone among you sick? Let them call the elders of the church to pray over them and anoint them with oil in the name of the Lord. And the prayer offered in faith will make the sick person well; the Lord will raise them up. If they have sinned, they will be forgiven. Therefore confess your sins to each other and pray for each other so that you may be healed. The prayer of a righteous person is powerful and effective.
—James 5:13–16 NIV

Social distancing sounds like the opposite of Christian community. How are we to be the Church body in isolation in our homes? Although this is an unprecedented time in our history, it shouldn't give us the excuse to disengage with our communities. It may look different, but it can be just as fruitful – especially with the technology we have available to us today.

James reminds us that we can still pray for others. He says if we have friends or family in trouble, let them pray. This is a perfect time to ask others how you can pray for them and, in turn, they will likely ask you the same thing. Take this time to engage with the Lord, and become a prayer warrior. Maybe this isn't something that you're used to, but I know the Lord will honor the time as He encourages us to pray for each other and bear each other's burdens.

Many of you may have a regular Bible study or prayer group you attend. Now that we can't gather in small groups, it may feel like you are missing that community. Perhaps you can still gather virtually, whether that's a phone call or a video conference. For years, I've participated in a Bible study where one of the members actually lives in another state. We bring her in on an iPad, and "pass her around the room" so she can stay involved in the conversation. At first it seemed kind of odd, but now we wouldn't have it any other way; it allows her to stay engaged in a small group while we get to have the honor of connecting with her each week.

The second part of this Scripture reminds us to sing songs of praise if we are happy. It may be hard to relate to this emotion of happiness right now, but I encourage you to praise the Lord because it will indeed make you feel happy. Worshipping the Lord and glorifying His name will bring great joy and will also help you not to think so much about the current situation. No matter what our circumstances are, you can take comfort in the fact that God doesn't change; He is the same yesterday and today. Praise Him for that!

Find a way to stay connected to your community. We need each other now more than ever to get through this! The Lord created us to be in relationship with each other; be intentional and lean toward your fellow Believers for support. The Lord will bless the time, and you may grow closer to each other and to Him as you are vulnerable about what you're each dealing with in this difficult season.

We all have an amazing chance to draw closer to the Lord and each other. How awesome it would be if we can come out of this time with even stronger communities than we had before!

Practical Takeaway: Create a prayer board, and pray consistently for those around you. Spend time worshipping the Lord each day. Find a way to stay engaged in your spiritual community through text, email, video calls, etc.

Thoughts, Reflections and Prayers:

Day 6
The Lord's Will in This Season

Now listen, you who say, "Today or tomorrow we will go to this or that city, spend a year there, carry on business and make money." Why, you do not even know what will happen tomorrow. What is your life? You are a mist that appears for a little while and then vanishes. Instead, you ought to say, "If it is the Lord's will, we will live and do this or that."
—James 4:13–15 NIV

It's hard to remember what life was like before COVID-19. It seems that every day, our minds are filled with thinking about the coronavirus and how it is affecting our lives. How we will get our groceries, how we will get to work, and how we will take care of our loved ones? It's interesting to see how our thoughts are so consumed about this one thing when before, we often spent a lot of time thinking of things that were way less important.

Many cities are in lockdown, and only essential businesses are allowed to be open. This is kind of how our thoughts and actions are as well. You may have shifted to focus on the most important or essential things – your family, your friends, and the most crucial needs to live. And the non-essential thoughts, such as clothing to wear, movies to see, what color to paint the house, where you're going to go on Saturday night, have vanished from your mind. These things are not bad, but our current situation definitely puts things into perspective.

I find myself realizing how much time I used to spend thinking about non-essential things. I also have noticed I am appreciating small things in life much more. Each day that I wake up is a blessing. Looking out my window and seeing a blue sky. Hearing a bird chirp in the distance. Smelling the morning air. Talking to my family and praising God for their health. Laughing with a friend over a video chat. Being in the comfort of my home. Having a job and working unto the Lord each day. Your small moments may be different depending on your situation, but I encourage you to be thankful that we have this time to focus our thoughts on the essential blessings, instead of the non-essential things.

In today's verse, James explains that there is no point in worrying about tomorrow. Clearly, no one even knows what tomorrow will bring. Instead, we should trust the Lord's will for our lives. It can seem scary to trust the Lord, especially in this crazy season. That's why so many people "panic buy" supplies – it allows them to feel in control amid a very uncontrollable situation. But the Lord is trustworthy! The Lord is not panic buying faith and trust from the heavenly shelves. He still has all authority and power and control.

In the phrase "if the Lord wills," the word "will' used is the Greek word, *thelo*, which can be translated as "purpose." This is a great reminder that we shouldn't worry about tomorrow; the Lord has a plan and a purpose for our lives, and we should trust Him. We shouldn't spend time planning and thinking about non-essentials, but, instead, focus on the Lord's essential purpose that He has for each one of our lives.

Practical Takeaway: List the essential blessings that you are more aware of each day. Focus on the present day, and live in the moment with the Lord.

Thoughts, Reflections and Prayers:

Day 7
Perseverance in Trials

Blessed is the one who perseveres under trial because, having stood the test, that person will receive the crown of life that the Lord has promised to those who love him.
—James 1:12 NIV

As you know, we count as blessed those who have persevered. You have heard of Job's perseverance and have seen what the Lord finally brought about. The Lord is full of compassion and mercy.
—James 5:11 NIV

As the last day of this journey into the book of James comes to a close, I want to draw your attention to these two verses, where James proclaims blessings for those who have persevered. The coronavirus is an invisible enemy, and it takes all of us doing our part to follow the guidelines and stay healthy and safe. We will persevere, and we will come out stronger on the other side.

The word "persevere" used in both of today's verses, is the Greek word, *hypomeno*. One of the translations of this word is "to remain," specifically, to persevere under misfortunes and trials, to hold fast to one's faith in Jesus and to endure bravely and calmly. I hope and pray that out of this season comes a strong army of Believers who held fast to Jesus and who endured bravely and calmly. What an amazing testimony that would be to the world around us of the unshakeable faith in Messiah.

At the beginning of James 5:11 is the phrase, "we count as blessed." This translates to the Greek word, *makarizo*. Interestingly, this word is only used twice in the entire Bible. The only other use is in Luke 1:48, where Mary says, "all generations will call me blessed." This was right after Mary found out she was going to give birth to Jesus. What great company we are in that when we endure and persevere, we will be blessed in this same way.

Not only will we be blessed, but James 1:12 states that for those who withstand the trial, they will receive the crown of life. This word "crown" is translated as a mark of righteousness given to genuine servants of Jesus. There are many in the Bible who withstood hardships, from Moses and Abraham to Peter and Paul. James specifically mentions Job, who is a great example as he endured many trials. Our lives may feel like the book of Job right now. The Greek word used to describe Job's endurance means patient endurance, steadfastness, and constancy. I pray those are the characteristics each of us develop during this time.

James 5 reminds us of a great promise we can cling to during these times: The Lord is full of compassion and mercy. As I've mentioned many times this week, the Lord doesn't change. Our circumstances may be changing constantly, but God remains the same. He is loving and kind, merciful and full of grace. He hasn't forgotten you, and He knows exactly what you are going through. Hold fast to His promises, and endure this trial along with Him, knowing you will be blessed.

Practical Takeaway: Write down the characteristics you want to display to the world during this season. Ask the Lord to help you develop these so you can proclaim His name to those around you.

Thoughts, Reflections and Prayers:

Hope from James

I am sure of this very thing – that He who began a good work in you will carry it on to completion until the Day of Messiah Yeshua.

—Philippians 1:6

Week 5

HOPE
FROM PHILIPPIANS

Theo Steinhauer
Spiritual Affairs Manager

Day 1
From the Beginning until Completion

I am SURE of this very thing – that He who began a GOOD work in you WILL carry it on to COMPLETION until the Day of Messiah Yeshua.
—Philippians 1:6, emphasis added

It is easy for the human heart to get discouraged during times of trial and to feel as though the difficult circumstances surrounding us are somehow hindering the work of God in our lives. However, the Scriptures paint a different reality in that, despite these circumstances, God is there, completing the good work He has faithfully started in our lives. We may not understand how these trials can possibly fit into God's plans, or how this is part of Him completing what He began in us, but we can rest assured that what is written in His Word is true and reliable.

God promises us that "all things work together for the good for those who love God and are called according to His purpose" (Romans 8:28). God also promises us in Proverbs 16:9 that "the heart of man plans his course, but Adonai directs his steps." These Scriptures should awaken in us an incredible sense of assurance in God's faithfulness towards we who believe and bring a certain level of hope and encouragement to our hearts. He is the good and faithful Shepherd of our lives. He will never leave us nor forsake us. He can be trusted throughout every circumstance, because He is the One who began the good work in us and will carry it on to completion. Yes, even now in the midst of this trial, He is completing the work He has started in each of us.

The Word of God is alive and active, speaking truth into our lives, helping us establish a firm foundation to stand on while we go through life on this side of eternity. Please take some time to quietly meditate on the passages above and ask yourself these three questions:

Hope from Philippians

What truth is being spoken in these passages?

What does this mean for me?

How should I respond?

Day 2
The Advancement of the Good News

Now I want you to know, brothers and sisters, that what has happened to me has actually resulted in the advancement of the Good News. And so, my imprisonment in the cause of Messiah has become well known throughout the Praetorian Guard and to everyone else. Because of my imprisonment, most of the brothers and sisters have become confident in the Lord to dare more than ever to speak the message fearlessly.
—Philippians 1:12–14

What incredible verses these are, reminding us that not even trials and tribulations can stop the work of the Lord! Often enough, when the Church faces opposition or difficult circumstances, causing our everyday lives as the body of Messiah to come to a halt, we tend to believe that the work of the Lord is being hindered in that moment. This creates feelings of discouragement and defeat, and in some cases even anger. All these can cause us to focus our attention in the wrong place. This is the very circumstance that the apostle Paul found himself in when he wrote to the church in Philippi.

Paul had been imprisoned by the Roman government for preaching and teaching the Good News of Yeshua, and the work of his ministry seemed to have come to a halt. However, we see in verse twelve of chapter one, that this opposition and very difficult situation "actually resulted in the advancement of the Good News" and Paul even states that, because of his imprisonment, "most of the brothers and sisters have become confident in the Lord to dare more than ever to speak the message fearlessly."

What Paul and the *kedoshim* (saints or holy ones) in Philippi were experiencing was the incredible grace and faithfulness of God to use His people as His witnesses in every circumstance of life. There is no circumstance that can stop the advancement of the Good News because God is faithful to make Himself known through those who love Him.

Today we find ourselves in a global pandemic, a pandemic that has caused churches, synagogues and ministries all over the world to close their doors and stop their usual ministry activities. But we must not be discouraged, not even for a minute, and think that the Good News is being hindered from advancing and changing people's lives. Let us read this example in the Word of God with confidence that the trials we are facing today will result in the advancement of the Good News. And let us become more confident in the Lord "to dare more than ever to speak the message fearlessly."

Reflecting on God's living and active Word

What truth is being spoken in these passages?

What does this mean for me?

How should I respond?

Day 3
Rejoicing Through Every Circumstance

Yes, and I will keep rejoicing, for I know that this will turn out for my deliverance, through your intercession and the help of the Ruach [Spirit] of Messiah Yeshua. My eager expectation and hope is that in no way will I be put to shame, but that with complete boldness Messiah will even now, as always, be exalted in my body—whether through life or through death. For to me, to live is Messiah and to die is gain.
—Philippians 1:18b–21

Yes, let *us* also keep rejoicing through every circumstance, because those who love the Lord will "in no way be put to shame." Why is that? How can Paul say this when he has been arrested, beaten and thrown into prison? How can we, as Believers, rejoice in every circumstance, not being ashamed of our lives in Messiah, when life all around us seems to be unraveling at the seams and death is knocking at our door? The answer lies in verse 21 of this passage, "For to me, to live is Messiah and to die is gain."

You see, the absolute reality for those who belong to Jesus is that, no matter what circumstance we find ourselves in here on this Earth, we live to magnify Yeshua. We live as His witnesses, proclaiming His Good News and His kingdom. Every day that we have on this Earth is an opportunity to know Him more, to be transformed into His likeness by the washing of the Word (Ephesians 5:26) and the power of the Holy Spirit, and to make Him known to others. It is a significant life of purpose and meaning.

Our life here on Earth is found in Messiah. It is orchestrated by Him, shepherded by Him, and empowered by His Spirit. No circumstance can remove us from His great love, not even death itself (Romans 8:38–39). This is why we will not be put to shame. This is why we can rejoice. While we are living on this Earth, Jesus is our source, and we are His witnesses. And when we die, we have the promise of being in His presence and the promise of the resurrection. We gain either way! Therefore, there is no shame for those who belong to Yeshua, neither in life nor in death. So, let us boldly stand on these truths and confidently say, "I will keep rejoicing, for I know that this will turn out for my deliverance.... For to me, to live is Messiah and to die is gain."

Reflecting on God's living and active Word

What truth is being spoken in these passages?

What does this mean for me?

How should I respond?

Day 4
The Lord's Great and Unfailing Love

Only live your lives in a manner worthy of the Good News of the Messiah. Then, whether I come and see you or I am absent, I may hear of you that you are standing firm in one spirit – striving side by side with one mind for the faith of the Good News and not being frightened in anyway by your opponents. For them this is a sign of destruction, but for you salvation—and that from God. For to you was granted for Messiah's sake not only to trust in Him, but also to suffer for His sake—experiencing the same struggle you saw in me and now you are hearing in me.
—Philippians 1:27–30

Fear is a powerful aspect of life that can render the strongest of individuals helpless. But as God's children, holy and dearly loved, we have the amazing gift of God's love that removes all fear. For the Scriptures say that "There is no fear in love, but perfect love drives out fear" (1 John 4:18).

Praise the Lord! This empowers us to live our "lives in a manner worthy of the Good News of the Messiah," even amid suffering and trials. This love is so great, so tangibly powerful and effective, that Paul could confidently say that, "For to you was granted for Messiah's sake not only to trust in Him, but also to suffer for His sake" – because he knows that God's love is sufficient to sustain us in the midst of suffering and that our lives, being lived out in a manner worthy of the Lord in the midst of trials, is a powerful and effective sign and witness. Hallelujah!

A sign and a witness to whom? Well, a sign and a witness to those who don't belong to the Lord and also a sign and witness of salvation to all those that do belong.

Therefore, since it has been granted to us as Believers to not only trust in this great Messiah but also to suffer under various trials and tribulations in this life, let us cling to His great, unfailing love.

Let us live our lives a manner that is worthy of the Good News of Yeshua in the midst of today's trying circumstances – in order to be the sign and witnesses He has called and graced us to be.

Reflecting on God's living and active Word

What truth is being spoken in these passages?

What does this mean for me?

How should I respond?

Day 5
Experiencing the Shalom of God

Rejoice in the Lord always—again I will say, rejoice!
—Philippians 4:4

Beholding the Lord and having your heart transformed by the reality of who He is, is undoubtedly one of the most powerful and life-changing aspects of life. If we want our lives to be transformed into the likeness of Yeshua our Messiah, if we desire to be strong in our faith and able to rejoice in the Lord always, in all circumstances, then we must give ourselves time to sit at His feet and meditate on His Word.

Right now, read through these passages, meditate on them, and ask the Holy Spirit to renew your mind as you read the Word of God. My prayer is that, by the end of your time, your mind will be renewed, your heart fully encouraged, and "the shalom of God, which surpasses all understanding, will guard your heart and mind in Messiah Yeshua."

> *Rejoice in the Lord always—again I will say, rejoice! Let your gentleness be known to all people. The Lord is near. Do not be anxious about anything—but in everything, by prayer and petition with thanksgiving, let your requests be made known to God.*
>
> *And the shalom [peace, completeness] of God, which surpasses all understanding, will guard your hearts and your minds in Messiah Yeshua. Finally, brothers and sisters, whatever is true, whatever is honorable, whatever is just, whatever is pure, whatever is lovely, whatever is commendable—if there is any virtue and if there is anything worthy of praise—dwell on these things. What you have learned and received and heard and seen in me—put these things into practice, and the God of shalom will be with you.*
> —Philippians 4:7–9

Hope from Philippians

What truth is being spoken in these passages?

What does this mean for me?

How should I respond?

Day 6
Abiding in Yeshua

I know what it is to live with humble means, and I know what it is to live in prosperity. In any and every circumstance I have learned the secret of contentment—both to be filled and to go hungry, to have abundance and to suffer need. I can do all things through Messiah who strengthens me.
—Philippians 4:12–13

According to the Word of God, we can do all things through Messiah who strengthens us. God's Word is true, trustworthy, and able to renew the human mind. Therefore, when it says that we can do all things through Him who gives us strength, this means that we, as followers of Yeshua, have this strength available to us to go through every single day of our lives. If this was not the case, then it would not have been written in Scripture.

This strength that enables us to face every moment that presents itself to us on any given day is available through Messiah and Messiah alone. Again, the secret to being content in all situations, to experiencing the shalom that surpasses our understanding, to rejoicing always, to walking in a manner worthy of the Good News in midst of dark and trying times, to focusing our thoughts on things above and not the things of the world, to having the strength to be able to do all things, is available to us in having an intimate relationship with Jesus the Messiah.

Yeshua says, "I am the vine, you are the branches, the one who abides in Me, and I in him, bears much fruit; for apart from Me, you can do nothing" (John 15:5).

Abiding in Yeshua is the secret to a successful life as a child of God. It is the only way for our lives to experience the glorious, life-giving fruits of the Holy Spirit in any and all circumstances. Let us abide in the vine, Jesus the Messiah, and only then will we find the strength to do all things for today – all the while producing the good fruit that comes from a life in God.

Reflecting on God's living and active Word

What truth is being spoken in these passages?

What does this mean for me?

How should I respond?

Day 7
Cultivating Encouragement in our Communities

Therefore, if there is any encouragement in Messiah, if there is any comfort of love, if there is any fellowship of the Ruach [Spirit], if there is any mercy or compassion, then make my joy complete by being of the same mind, having the same love, united in spirit, with one purpose. Do nothing out of selfishness or conceit, but with humility, consider others as more important than yourselves, looking not only to your own interest but also for the interest of others. Have this attitude in yourselves, which also was in Messiah Yeshua.
—Philippians 2:1–5

The human heart will respond in various ways during difficult and life-changing circumstances. However, regardless of how our hearts respond, the Lord is always there to help. When we have fellowship with Him, we experience encouragement and comfort from His love. When we respond to life in unexpected ways and our sins and weaknesses are exposed, He demonstrates abundant mercy and compassion towards us who believe. This is the amazing grace and love of our God and Savior Yeshua, and we will do well to follow the example of our Messiah.

Therefore, as we face today's challenging times, let us respond to each other as Jesus responds to us. Let us create an environment of compassion, comfort, love, and encouragement both in our homes and in our communities, just as Jesus does for us through His Holy Spirit and His Word. Let's not look out for our own interests alone, but also for the interests of others and, in doing so, have the attitude in ourselves, which also was in Messiah Yeshua.

Reflecting on God's living and active Word

What truth is being spoken in these passages?

What does this mean for me?

How should I respond?

Trust in the LORD forever, for the LORD, the LORD himself, is the Rock eternal.

—Isaiah 26:4 NIV

Week 6

HOPE
FROM ISAIAH

Leah Aviva
Children's Education Program Manager
& Community Liaison

Day 1
More Than Bread

We are living in uncertain times. Over the last weeks, the world has been thrown into a whirlwind of panic and fear. The fear of sickness, loss and grief has overwhelmed many of us. Also, startling has been the worry about medical supplies and household resources. It would be natural to ask, *Lord, where are You? Is this our new normal? What is my role in Your kingdom today?*

The prophet Isaiah had experience living in troubling times too. At first, the people of Israel were worshiping false idols and rebelling against God's covenant. Isaiah warned them that if they did not repent, judgment would come through the rise of Assyria and Israel's ultimate exile to Babylon. But the story of Israel shows us that God's judgment was not the final outcome; His plan for salvation was sovereignly at work, and He was always with His people.

Later in history, Isaiah reminds us that there is hope and comfort. We can have a positive, cheerful expectation of something good – hope for all who repent and trust in the Lord. His message was simple, return to Jerusalem where God Himself will bring His kingdom to pass through His Servant King, and all nations will see His glory. The people were not merely to return to Jerusalem physically, but to inwardly turn their hearts fully over to the Lord, to follow Him and obey His ways.

> *...In returning and rest you shall be saved; in quietness and confidence shall be your strength.*
> —Isaiah 30:15a NKJV

From this posture of relationship and rest, the people could extend God's mercy and grace to others in times of need. We have a great hope that in times of darkness, God's light and love can shine out of us. The Lord promises to always provide for us, guide, strengthen and protect us as we give of our material and spiritual resources to comfort those around us.

> *The LORD will guide you continually, And satisfy your soul in drought, And strengthen your bones; You shall be like a watered garden, And like a spring of water, whose waters do not fail.*
> —Isaiah 58:11 NKJV

Thoughts, Reflections and Prayers:

Day 2
Purified for Purpose

Don't you love good news? Now, more than ever, hearing a happy ending or an uplifting report has become especially newsworthy and poignant.

Isaiah was entrusted as a messenger to the people of Israel, and he pleaded that they humble themselves and fear the Lord. He reported that Israel was in danger of being destroyed and that if they would not turn from their rebellion, judgment would be coming. This was bad news, and undoubtedly the people wanted to change the channel.

> "...Destruction has been decreed, overwhelming and righteous."
> —Isaiah 10:22 NIV

Yet, what seemingly looked like a dead end for Jerusalem was really a beginning. God judged the city of Jerusalem by bringing the nations to conquer it – for a divine purpose: to purify Israel from wickedness and injustice. The Lord would never abandon His promises to Abraham, and yet, this was not a license for the people of Israel to sin.

The Lord was waiting on Israel to trust in Him and turn from evil. Out of God's great love and compassion, Israel's story does not end with destruction and judgment. This was good news and there was hope.

> *"For a brief moment I abandoned you, but with deep compassion I will bring you back. In a surge of anger I hid my face from you for a moment, but with everlasting kindness I will have compassion on you," says the Lord your Redeemer.*
> —Isaiah 54:7–8 NIV

Much like a purifying fire that burns away impurities, God's judgment of fire helped remove worthless things from Israel in order to make room for the good. The Lord used an intense and painful purification process to restore Jerusalem. He was moving in the hearts of the people of Israel to make them fit for purpose – to bring delight and honor to Him and be a reflection on the Earth of His mercy and redemption. God's judgment was never the final word. His end game is always good – our purification – in order to redeem, give hope, bring peace and justice to all that would call on His name.

> *...who says of Jerusalem, "It shall be inhabited, of the towns of Judah, "They shall be rebuilt,' and of their ruins, "I will restore them..."*
>
> —Isaiah 44:26b NIV

Reflection

Are there any places in your life that you are experiencing the fire of purification? Lift up anything that comes to your mind, and ask God for help to submit to His process, knowing He will bring good. Ask for a soft heart to learn all He may wish to show you through such a fiery trial.

Are there any places in your life that are not fully surrendered to the Lord? Do you sense any resistance in your heart to fully trust Him?

How might God be using difficulties to deepen your love and hope in Him?

Day 3
Beyond Roadblocks

Before embarking on a journey, we hope there will be no delays, detours or accidents. It's only natural that we want to take the path of least resistance. *How long will it take to arrive? Is this the most direct route? Is there a shortcut?* We want to do whatever is necessary to get to our destination quickly, unencumbered and without expense.

God provided the people of Israel with a covenant promise – a one-way, non-stop ticket to a life of hope and peace. Israel's role was to not be idle passengers, but to trust the Lord, turn from false worship and be a witness to all around them of their faithful and loving God. But there were roadblocks – barriers of doubt, sin and rebellion – that delayed their arrival and ability to receive salvation.

During the prophet Isaiah's time, Israel's people were living in sin. They had forgotten the many marvelous works God had done for them, and their hearts had become hardened. They didn't want to keep God's commandments, and they became weary living under oppression.

Israel's rescue was not happening according to their timetable or strength. Yet, because of the Lord's great faithfulness and love to keep His covenant to them, their delay would soon be over. God spoke through Isaiah and reminded them that He was doing a new thing, that He was going to turn away all ungodliness from Jacob and bring forth the Messiah who is the water of life. The people were beckoned to hope against hope and look forward to the promised Servant King who would, in due season, reconcile all mankind to the living God and bring salvation to the nations.

> *I bring My righteousness near, it shall not be far off; My salvation shall not linger. And I will place salvation in Zion, for Israel My glory.*
> —Isaiah 46:13 NKJV

Reflection
In times of uncertainty and when our feathers get ruffled, what comes out of you?

Is there anything in your life that is blocking your ability to fully yield and trust in the Lord? Are there any roadblocks of sin and doubt in your life today?

How might the Lord be inviting you to repent and cast your burdens onto Him?

Day 4
Holy Boldness

Isaiah was a visionary. He lived in Jerusalem near the end of Israel's kingdom period. It was a time of unrest, and yet, his life was marked by prophetic vision. On the Lord's behalf, Isaiah spoke boldly to the leaders of Jerusalem in a way that would impact the entire community. Can you imagine the weight of that responsibility?

Isaiah's dreams and visions concerning Israel were extensive and profound. The people were rebelling against their covenant with God, and they were in great danger. Isaiah had the unpopular task of warning them that God would judge the community if they continued worshiping false idols and oppressing the poor.

> *I revealed Myself to those who did not ask for Me...*
> —Isaiah 65:1a NIV

Isaiah had the gift of holy boldness, and his messages pointed far beyond his own day. Despite not seeing God's promises come to pass in his lifetime, Isaiah trusted in God, and that gave him courage. In the face of continual rejection by the leaders of Jerusalem, Isaiah, compelled by heavenly hope, urged the people of Israel to repent and turn to the Lord. He was devoted and bold to speak out and intercede on Israel's behalf despite personal consequence.

> *I have not spoken in secret...I did not say to the seed of Jacob, "Seek Me in vain..."*
> —Isaiah 45:19 NKJV

Although the people were headed for ruin, Isaiah never stopped declaring God's words that spoke of the New Jerusalem – where all death and suffering would end. Isaiah pointed the people to remember the faithfulness of God and His covenant promises – the punishment would not last forever. Instead, through the forthcoming King, the Lord Himself would rule and reign over a redeemed people with all justice and mercy.

> *Trust in the LORD forever, for the LORD, the LORD himself, is the Rock eternal.*
> —Isaiah 26:4 NIV

Isaiah was one of Israel's greatest prophets, and he boldly testified in a critical time in Israel's history. He beckoned the people to soften their hearts and trust in the coming Messiah, the hope of Israel. Isaiah's life vision reminds us of his daring hope in the Lord – and that we can boldly trust in God's promise to redeem, rescue and renew us.

Reflection:
Do you have a vision to minister to people in your life, family and community?

How might God be inviting you to be bold and to fulfill His kingdom purposes today?

Identify any obstacles that may be blocking your ability to walk in boldness for the Lord. Pray, confess and receive God's love and grace today to strengthen your personal life vision.

Day 5
A Stump of Hope

In the early chapters of Isaiah, hope seems lost. Israel is falling deeper into disobedience and inching closer to a place of no return. Their hearts were hardened to God's ways, and they sink more each day toward the ocean floor. Were all things lost for the people of Israel?

In this setting, Isaiah was commissioned to take a stand of faith and trust in the Lord – to declare with authority that God is a sovereign, righteous judge who has set the nation of Israel apart to be a witness of His glory throughout the Earth. Yet, the picture Isaiah paints is foreboding. Isaiah receives a vision that depicts Israel being chopped down like a tree and left like a stump in a field. If that wasn't grim enough, Isaiah went on to share that this stump would also be burned with fire until all that is left is ashes.

Are there circumstances in your life that have left you feeling hardened and broken?

What seemed like a neglected garden, decimated to ashes, held a promise within. After the burning and purification by fire, out of the smoldering stump would be a Holy Seed, a future sign of hope. The Lord would be faithful to the promises He made to David – He would send a new King to arise from an old stump, and set His people free.

> *"For He grew up before Him like a tender shoot, and like a root out of parched ground; He had no stately form or majesty that we should look upon Him, nor appearance that we should be attracted to Him."*
> —Isaiah 53:2 NASB

This King would be empowered by God's Spirit to rule and reign over a New Jerusalem and transform the world with justice and wisdom.

> *A shoot will come up from the stump of Jesse; from His roots a Branch will bear fruit...In that day the Root of Jesse will stand as a banner for the peoples; the nations will rally Him, and His resting place will be glorious.*
> —Isaiah 11:1, 10 NIV

All was not lost for Israel. Where there was only a heap of ashes and a rotting stump, salvation would emerge through the coming Messiah. God's faithfulness to Israel compels us to hope in His promises.

Let us align our hearts with Yeshua – to believe that out of ashes, out of every single life circumstance, a great and eternal hope can arise.

Pray for the Lord to strengthen your resolve to choose hope. When all we may see is a deserted garden, God promises to make something new, to heal and be a refuge for all. He has done and will continue to do great things out of a stump!

Reflection
Are there areas in your life that are dry and need reviving?

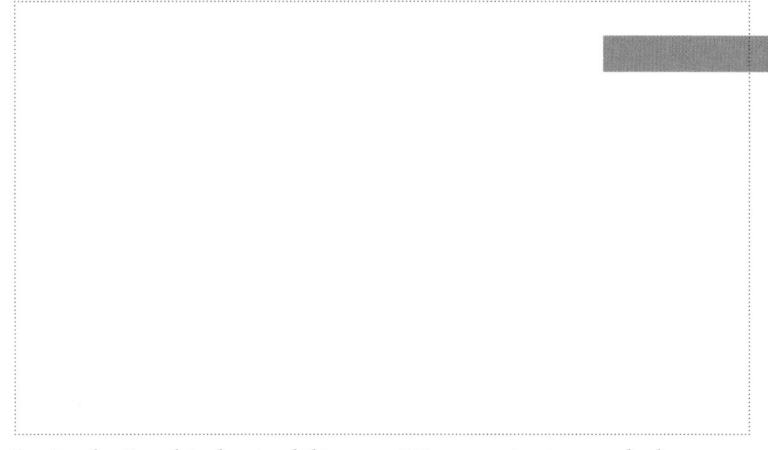

Invite the Lord today to deliver on His promise to touch that very place with His Spirit and power.

Day 6
Covenant Family

The nation of Israel is a divine archetype of purpose and family. God fashioned Israel to be a witness of His persistent love and righteousness. Israel was to be a servant and a reflection to all the nations of the Lord's covenant promise to redeem the world from sin and unrighteousness. They were to show the world He is the one true God, the maker of Heaven and Earth.

> *"I, the LORD, have called You in righteousness... I will keep You and will make You to be a covenant for the people and a light for the Gentiles, to open eyes that are blind...to release from the dungeon those who sit in darkness."*
> —Isaiah 42:6–7 NIV

> *But now, thus says the LORD, who created you, O Jacob, and He who formed you, O Israel... "I have called you by your name; you are Mine."*
> —Isaiah 43:1 NKJV

Throughout the book of Isaiah, we are reminded of God's desire to provide consolation and comfort to His people. Though they had been cast into exile, the Lord's purposes to deliver, protect and restore their identity prevails. The thread of our Creator's nature as a compassionate, merciful, faithful, loving Father is woven deeply into history of the birth of Israel and the nations – a covenant family.

Deep within the heart of God is a desire for His children to know Him as a Father and know their identity as His children. Isaiah tells us that, through repentance, the humble will inherent the New Jerusalem and be entirely renewed as His creation. This is true for Gentile and Jewish Believers in Messiah.

If you were born, you are meant to be part of God's family – to know Him as Creator and Redeemer. Isaiah reminds us that God created a covenant family of all nations who are awaiting the hope of His justice to the world. As a member of the household of Israel or joined as His inheritance from the nations, we are all the Lord's family.

Reflection
How might God be inviting you to know Him more deeply as a member of His family today?

Is there anything keeping you from experiencing His nearness as a loving Father?

Consider calling a brother or sister in the Lord to talk and pray with them about this. Who might you call? Write about your conversation.

Day 7
Rest & Living Water

A celebrated tradition in Messianic Jewish culture is gathering around the table and breaking bread with family, friends and even strangers. This weekly rhythm of Shabbat dinner provides both structure and comfort to stop all customary work, take a deep breath and enter into the Lord's rest. Shabbat is an inheritance to remember God's creation and receive His peace. Every week, Believers have an open invitation to come, sit at the table and feast on the Good News of Yeshua that compels us to hope for His return.

Isaiah reminds us that his greatest hope for Israel was that they would repent and turn to faithfully worship the Lord. He longed to see the New Jerusalem where God's kingdom would be restored through the future Messiah, who would then bring all nations together in peace. He warned Israel that those who thirsted and depended on their own strength to earn righteousness would never find rest, they would never be satisfied.

> *Come, all you who are thirsty, come to the waters...*
> —Isaiah 55:1 NIV

Each of us have a canyon of needs and longings, yet there is great comfort and hope in God's steadfast love and faithfulness. Those who recognize their thirst, their need for forgiveness and salvation, are invited to drink from living waters – waters purchased by the atoning sacrifice of the Messiah.

> *The work of righteousness will be peace, And the service of righteousness will be quietness and confidence forever.*
> —Isaiah 32:17 NASB

The cost of this offering is too high a thing for most of us to grasp, but we are not helpless nor hopeless. We have choices every day to part with sin and recognize our need for God to fill our hearts with a hope that can be only satisfied in Him. We each long for deep peace that brings rest to our souls. Before we can receive salvation, we must see our need for it.

Remember, it's God's supernatural work of righteousness alone that brings true peace – freedom from the guilt and weight of sin.

> *Let the wicked forsake his way and the unrighteous man his thoughts; And let him return to the LORD, And He will have compassion on him; And to our God, For He will abundantly pardon.*
> —Isaiah 55:7 NASB

Reflection

When is the last time you stopped and took a deep breath? Try this centering prayer: As you inhale say, "Abba," and on exhaling say, "I belong to you." Repeat as needed, and enter into His rest. Write about your experience.

Are there areas in your life that need living waters? Share those longing and needs in prayer as you reflect now.

What is the role of repentance in your life? How might repentance help you receive greater peace and hope from the Lord today?

Now may the God of hope fill you with all joy and peace in believing, that you may abound in hope by the power of the Holy Spirit.

—Romans 15:13 NKJV

Week 7

HOPE
FROM ROMANS

Rabbi Troy Wallace
Vice President of Congregation
& Leadership Development

Day 1
Hoping Against All Reason

Therefore it is of faith that it might be according to grace, so that the promise might be sure to all the seed, not only to those who are of the law, but also to those who are of the faith of Abraham, who is the father of us all… who, contrary to hope, in hope believed, so that he became the father of many nations, according to what was spoken, "So shall your descendants be."
—Romans 4:16, 18 NKJV

Sometimes our hope as those who are of the God of Abraham is "contrary to hope." Our hope is against all reason to hope. Our hope is against all odds, despite the circumstances and just doesn't make any sense. Even when the world around us would tell us that all hope is lost, we have reason and confidence to hope.

Let's consider Abraham as Paul does in this passage from the fourth chapter of his letter to the Romans. Abraham was 75 years old, and his wife was 65, when the Lord first made a promise to him about being "a great nation" (Genesis 12:2). When he was 99 years old, the Lord promised him that he would be "a father of many nations" (Genesis 17:4). Abraham and Sarah had been committed to trying to have children through all of their "most fruitful" childbearing years. They had been walking in a promise for 24 years that had not come to pass. In terms of the natural life cycle, the hope for children was all but gone.

I know many couples who have found themselves in similar circumstances. It has tested their marriages and tested their faith. It did for Abraham and Sarah as well. They tried doing different things to bring it about (Genesis 16). They laughed at the idea (Genesis 17:7, 18:12). They asked the Lord if He was sure that He would do what He promised (Genesis 15:2–3). But Abraham and Sarah were unusual. When the Lord Almighty made them a promise of children, even in the dusk of their lives, Abraham believed (Genesis 15:6). He chose hope and not despair.

Paul encouraged the Romans, many of whom are not from a Jewish background, to take upon themselves the unusual hope of Abraham. A hope that sustains faith by grace even when every circumstance in life would tell us to believe we should be hopeless. That is a hope that brings new life into our circumstances, our families and our world.

Our world has changed in light of the COVID-19 pandemic. Our patterns of life have been altered. But there is reason to hope. We serve a promise-keeping God! And we have models of faith like Abraham and Sarah on page after page of the Scriptures. May we be people who, "contrary to hope, in hope believe"!

Activation
List all the reasons NOT to hope in your life today. Be honest.

Now speak them out loud and declare after each one, "I will hope!" Write down any thoughts you have about your experience.

Day 2
From Trouble to Hope

*And not only that, but we also glory in tribulations,
knowing that tribulation produces perseverance;
and perseverance, character; and character, hope.*
—Romans 5:3–4 NKJV

Paul explained to the Romans that the development of hope in our lives is a process. There are four elements: tribulation, perseverance, character and hope. They work together in three steps:

1. Tribulation produces perseverance
2. Perseverance produces character
3. Character produces hope

Hope is developed in us by a process. Helping the Romans understand this process and how to anticipate and respond to it is the goal of Paul's encouragement.

I love hope! It makes it easy for me to find joy. When I am hopeful, I often am able to be excited, and even giddy. But what produces hope – the parts of the process – those words make me feel something different. Perhaps words like "tribulation" or "perseverance" create the same internal or emotional response for you.

Tribulation produces perseverance
My approach to life is generally one that seeks to avoid tribulation. But Paul encourages the community of Believers in Rome to approach tribulation by expecting it be productive in their lives. He is, in some ways saying, "As Believers in Jesus, let's view tribulation as an opportunity. Tribulation will produce perseverance, that is patience, in you."

What a different point of view! What if we were to let our internal response to tribulation be, "I can't wait to see how much patience this is going to produce in me!"? And as perseverance is developed in response to tribulation, our mindset might just change in response to trials and troubles in our lives. May it be so!

Perseverance produces character
If we can adjust our view on tribulation and see patience and perseverance grow, Paul assures us that character follows. Character is our whole person – the way we think, feel and behave. If we allow troubles to produce patience, our character is formed. Our whole person is bettered because of patience, because of challenges in life. Perseverance in the face of tribulation produces a character in us that emanates and radiates the qualities of the Lord we serve. He was patient in the face of trouble and even death. And He endured it all for our sake. May we be the same way. Let us allow His character to be produced in us when we face challenges in the world and in our lives.

Character produces hope
With our moral and mental attributes in the likeness of the Messiah, hope is the expected outcome. With our character fully formed and established, our disposition becomes one that is predisposed to hope. Even when things are hard. Even when everyone else around us is hopeless. Hope, as an outcome of tribulation – what a stunning thought and brilliant insight. And an unusual approach.

If we go back to the beginning of this verse, I think Paul shows us a key to how the hope process works. He describes a "pre-condition" or "pre-disposition" that activates the process leading to hope. He says, "we also glory in tribulations" as the pre-amble to the process. Our assumption related to trouble and challenges must be that we are going to "glory" in them. Excuse me? Can you say that again? I think I misunderstood you. We *glory* in tribulation. Why? Because our expectation is that hope will be the outcome. May it be so with us and with you. Today, in this season and always!

Activation

Are you facing opportunities for perseverance in your life in this season? What are they?

Is patience your expected outcome of trouble?

In what ways is the Lord challenging your character in this season?

Are you inclined to hope? What is your expectation of troubles in life?

Day 3
Hope Does Not Disappoint

Now hope does not disappoint, because the love of God has been poured out in our hearts by the Holy Spirit who was given to us.
—Romans 5:5 NKJV

As we continue to discover Paul's exhortation to hope in his writing to the Romans, let us consider his thoughts in verse 5 of the fifth chapter. And I want to look at it in reverse order.

The Holy Spirit has been given to us
I wonder, do we take this incredible truth for granted as followers of Jesus the Messiah? The essence of the Lord's glory and of who He is have been granted to us. The Spirit of His own holiness is available to us. Because Jesus freely gave His life and put on hold His earthly kingdom on the throne of David, our heavenly Father sent the Spirit as a gift that we can depend on. What a blessed reality. What an incredible gift!

The love of God has been poured out in our hearts
Just as His Spirit has been given to us, His love has been poured out in our hearts. Sometimes in our culture, love can be fleeting. Marriages grow cold. Romance becomes fickle. But our God's love is not fleeting, cold or fickle. It is poured out – even to overflowing – in our hearts. There is not "just enough love" to make it work – there is extra. An abundance. It overflows. This kind of love overwhelms us with a sense of value, a sense of belonging and a sense of security. Jesus demonstrated this kind of love in how He lived and how He died. And the Father assured us of this kind of love in raising Jesus up from the dead. May we live in the fullness of His love!

Hope does not disappoint
With the closeness of His Spirit and the fullness of His love, we have a hope that does not disappoint. We may go through life and find ourselves disappointed as our circumstances change

and our dreams are left unfulfilled. But the hope of God's love by His Spirit does not disappoint all that He promises. Our faith demonstrates hope by grace despite the challenges of our situation and the presence of trouble and setbacks – because we know that one day Jesus will come in His fullness and make things right in our world. His hope by His Spirit and in His love does not disappoint. Allow His hope to be renewed in you today!

Activation
What are you disappointed about? Write it down. Make a list.

As you reflect on these disappointments, how can you invite the love of the Lord, by His Spirit, to renew your hope?

Speak those disappointments out loud and ask that God renew your hope today.

Day 4
Waiting with Eager Hope

...hope that is seen is not hope; for why does one still hope for what he sees? But if we hope for what we do not see, we eagerly wait for it with perseverance...
—Romans 8:24–25 NKJV

I want to encourage you to take a moment, and read the verse above a couple more times. Paul is using logic here to point out to the Roman community of Jesus followers that if we see with our eyes what we hope for, then there is no longer a need for hope. If our hope comes to pass, there is left no reason to hope. Only *before* something happens or comes to pass can hope be alive and active. A hopeful life is superior in every way. But hope is only of any consequence if what we desire to occur has not occurred yet.

What is our ultimate hope as followers of Jesus? Our hope is the same as the hope of the prophets of Israel – that the Son of David would come and establish an everlasting kingdom of justice and peace that extends over all (Isaiah 2:1–4, Isaiah 11, Habakkuk 2:9–20, Revelation 19:11–22:5). Jesus said to the disciples that He would come and do just that in the Father's time (Acts 1:6–7). Paul tells the community of faith in Corinth in his first letter that "[Jesus] must reign until He puts all enemies under His feet" (1 Corinthians 15:25). Jesus will come and make Jerusalem a praise in all the Earth (Isaiah 62:7). And because we do not see it yet, we have hope for the day that we will.

As we are waiting, how should we wait? We wait eagerly. We wait with perseverance. Eagerness is the quality of wanting or longing for something very much – with great anticipation, with keen expectancy and with invested interest. We are interested in Jesus' kingdom being fully present on the Earth. We desire His kingdom to come and His will to be done on the Earth as it is in Heaven (Matthew 6:10).

Perseverance is the quality of being persistent in doing or believing something despite difficulty or delay in achieving its success. We do not yet see His kingdom in its fullness – we do hope for it. And we wait with a keen expectancy despite His literal kingdom being delayed and the difficulty in establishing its ultimate success. And yet we hope eagerly and patiently for that which we do not see. With hope we cry, "Come Lord Jesus!" (Revelation 22:20).

Activation
What are some of your hopes that have come to pass in the course of your life?

What hopes are yet unfulfilled?

Are you good at waiting? Why or why not?

Day 5
A Stronger Hope

Rejoicing in hope, patient in tribulation,
continuing steadfastly in prayer.
—Romans 12:12 NKJV

In his sermon recorded in Ecclesiastes 4:12, Solomon states "though one may be overpowered by another, two can withstand him. And a threefold cord is not quickly broken." Solomon is writing of the value of camaraderie and relationships. I think we can apply Solomon's principle of multiplied strength through combining individual strengths to this passage in Romans chapter 12. Hope by itself is good. Hope braided together with joy, patience and prayer is even better.

Continuing steadfastly in prayer
Prayer is conversation with the Lord, God Most High. It is a natural result of our ongoing relationship with Him. Sometimes prayer is for giving thanks. Sometimes it is for making a request. Other times, it is simply a means of reinforcing our connection to God. Paul encouraged the Romans to pray steadfastly; that is, with constant attention. Our confidence in our relationship with the Lord of the universe serves to strengthen our hope. Regular and steady prayer will also serve to strengthen our hope.

Patient in tribulation
In Romans 5:3–4, Paul develops for the Romans what we have discussed as "the process of hope" (see Day Two). Experiencing tribulation, Paul tells us, should produce in us patience. Here in chapter 12, Paul is reminding the community of Jesus' disciples in Rome of this by exhorting them that as we experience tribulation and trouble, our response should be a patient one. We can wait on the LORD expectantly in the midst of trouble – He will deliver us. We can be patient in our trust of Him. Patience in combination with prayer will reinforce our hope in our good Lord.

Rejoicing in hope

To be hopeful is to have a confident expectation that something that has not happened will happen at some time in the future. Built into our hope is the reality that what we hope for has not *yet* come to pass (see Day 4). While we are waiting, what should our disposition be? Paul encourages us to *rejoice* while we wait. That is not my natural disposition. I dislike waiting. I avoid lines and traffic. I use self-checkout and the drive-thru to avoid waiting. But Paul tells us not only to have patience in the waiting, but to rejoice while we are hopeful. Joy strengthens our hope and enables us to pleasantly endure as we continue to hope for what is "not yet" to, one day, happen.

Prayer, patience and joy – a threefold cord that strengthens our hope. May it be so in us, Lord Jesus, today.

Activation

How is your prayer life?

Do you need more patience?

Does joy well up in your soul as you hope for the things He has promised?

If you find yourself to be deficient of any of these, take a moment and pray, asking that the Lord would strengthen these in you for the benefit of hope in Him. What is the Lord saying to you?

Day 6
Hope and Comfort in the Scriptures

*For whatever things were written before were written for our
learning, that we through the patience and comfort of
the Scriptures might have hope.*
—Romans 15:4 NKJV

If we are struggling to live from hope, take a look at Paul's encouragement to the Romans. He pointed them to look to the Scriptures to find hope. The record of testimony to the Lord's faithfulness to the people of Israel strengthens our hope today. In the Scriptures, Paul tells us we can find patience. In the Scriptures, Paul exhorts us that we can find comfort.

In his letter to the community of faith in Jesus in Galatia, Paul tells them that patience is a fruit of the Holy Spirit (Galatians 5:22). Patience is the by-product of our character having been re-formed by the indwelling Spirit of the living God. We can lean on the Holy Spirit for patience. And we can feed the Spirit's activity in us with the Scriptures. We can look to the Scriptures to build up patience in us – patience that leads to hope.

In the fortieth chapter of Isaiah, the prophet cries out, נחמו נחמו עמי – *nachamu, nachamu ami* – "comfort, comfort my people!" in the voice of the Lord (Isaiah 40:1). So often, the lives we lead are filled with trauma and doubt and hardship. Jesus tells us, "blessed are those who mourn for they shall be comforted" (Matthew 5:4). Paul is telling us, when we are in need of comfort, let us look to the Scriptures. Page after page and story after story declares the goodness of the God we serve. Look to the Scriptures and find comfort today!

Are you struggling to find hope? Look to the Scriptures, which were written for our learning, that you might find their comfort and that your patience might be built up. With patience and comfort reinforced in us, we can be built up in hope!

Activation
What is something that has happened to you and from which you still need comfort?

Do a simple word search of "comfort" in a Bible software, and read five of the chapters where that word occurs.

What jumped out as you read about comfort? How can the things that you read be applied to the area of comfort that you seek?

Day 7
Filled with Hope and Joy

Now may the God of hope fill you with all joy and peace in believing, that you may abound in hope by the power of the Holy Spirit.
—Romans 15:13 NKJV

Our God is the God of hope! As Paul draws to a close his treatise to the Roman community of faith in Jesus, he invokes the Lord as the God of hope. Inside of His own existence, there is hope. Though He is the God of all things, Paul highlights that He is the God of hope specifically. That should be an encouragement to us! Let us consider this together in our last devotion this week.

As the God of hope, He can fill us with all joy and peace – what a tremendous promise! *All* joy – not just some joy! Joy is a heart response to life that is independent of our circumstances. James says in the first chapter of his letter to Believers in Jesus from the first century that we should "consider it all joy when [we] encounter various trials…" (James 1:2). The God of hope can fill us with joy even when we face trouble and challenges. Hope from God can fill us with all joy!

Peace, too, is independent of circumstances. And Paul prays the God of hope will fill us with it as well. In John 16, Jesus tells His disciples of trouble ahead of time so that they might know it and prepare for it in their hearts. He makes them a promise of trouble but also promises them peace in the midst of it. He says, "These things I have spoken to you, that in Me you may have peace. In the world you will have tribulation; but be of good cheer, I have overcome the world" (John 16:33 NKJV). The God of hope promises a peace in us that is full.

Paul's instruction continues: "in believing." The gifts of joy and peace from the God of hope must be maintained in believing. "Believing" as Paul uses it here (and elsewhere) is not giving mental ascent to theological constructs. "Believing" is active – when worry presses against our minds, we confess with our mouths that "[our Lord] has not given us a spirit of fear but of power and of love and of a sound mind" (2 Timothy 1:7). Our believing creates an environment in our hearts and minds where the God of hope fills us with joy and peace. We believe that He works all things together for good for those who love Him and are called according to His purpose (Romans 8:28).

Our hope is not "barely hanging on." In Paul's declaration to the Roman community of faith, he describes our hope as one that abounds. Ours is a hope that exists in large amounts. It overflows. And when our hope abounds, it can affect the environment around us. It can be contagious. An inexplicable, abundant hope affords us many an opportunity to explain to a hopeless world the source of our abounding hope. Bless the Lord for a hope that abounds!

Lastly, Paul attributes this abounding hope –from the joy and peace of the God of hope in whom we believe – to the power of the Holy Spirit. This is not something we just decide or try to muster up in our own personality and emotions or as an act of our will. As the Holy Spirit empowers us to live in nearness to the Lord, He also empowers us to be filled with hope. We trust Him to pour out His power in us. That power becomes an abounding hope. Lord, may it be so with us!

Now, may the God of hope fill *you* with all joy and peace in these days. And as your believing is enriched, may you, by the power of the Holy Spirit, abound in hope! A hope that overflows. A hope that overwhelms. A hope that overcomes discouragement. A hope that builds you up. May the hope of the God of hope flourish in your heart and mind by the Messiah Jesus.

Activation
Has your hope been strengthened in this last week? If not, why not? Be specific.

If your hope has been strengthened, write down why and how so that you can look back on this in future times of worry or doubt and be encouraged.

If your hope has not been strengthened, write down where you still need a touch from the God of hope. Talk to the Lord about it. Don't be embarrassed, but do keep pressing into the promise of His hope abounding in you.

Therefore, take up the full armor of God, so that you may be able to resist when the times are evil, and after you have done everything, to stand firm. Stand firm then!

—Ephesians 6:13–14a

HOPE
FROM EPHESIANS

Week 8

Eric Pires
Associate Director of Global Operations

Day 1
Hope in His Calling

If you're like me, you love reminders. I have them everywhere. My workspace is full of sticky notes reminding me of tasks. My phone is set to remind me of birthdays, anniversaries and when to pay bills. I even have a reminder to check my reminders. Chapter 1 of Ephesians serves as our reminder of who we are in Messiah and how Mighty our God is. The Apostle Paul reminds followers of Jesus of two foundational truths.

First, our value is grounded in Messiah.

> *Blessed be the God and Father of our Lord Yeshua the Messiah, who has blessed us with every spiritual blessing in the heavenly places in Messiah. He chose us in the Messiah before the foundation of the world, to be holy and blameless before Him in love. He predestined us for adoption as sons through Messiah Yeshua, in keeping with the good pleasure of His will—to the glorious praise of His grace, with which He favored us through the One He loves!*
>
> —Ephesians 1:3–6

The second reminder has to do with Jesus' status and position, and who our Messiah really is (Ephesians 1:15–23). He is the Son of God. He is seated at the right hand of the Father. He is above any ruler, authority, power, leader and every other name that is named! All things have been placed under His feet and He has been appointed head over all things for His community. In a nutshell, I'm reminded that no matter the circumstances we find ourselves in, we serve an awesome God. And, through His Son, we are highly favored, blessed, adopted into His family, and have the Holy Spirit as a down payment of our promised inheritance as sons and daughters.

Do you need reminding of who you are in Messiah?

Is there anyone in your life that you can encourage with this identity reminder?

Can you receive the identity the Lord has given you? What is hindering you from receiving this truth?

Day 2
We are His Workmanship

My wife and I have three children. While we have been blessed to watch all three grow and mature, our middle child has been an interesting case study for me. Over the last two years, she has gone from a very talkative child, who depended on us to help her to do the smallest tasks, to a strong minded, independent young woman who loves Jesus and is still very talkative. While her outward appearance is the same, inwardly she has become something new.

The Apostle Paul outlines, in Ephesians chapter 2, the fact that while our outward appearance looks the same to the world, we have undergone an inward transformation through the mercy, grace and love of God through our relationship with Jesus. During the last 90 days, when so many of the things I've learned to love have been shut down or taken away, I have been able to rest in the fact that God has and continues to shape me from the inside, and no amount of physical distancing can change that. While the world has been turned upside down, we as followers of Jesus, can rest in the fact that our inward man has a foundation that can't be shaken.

> *You have been built on the foundation made up of the emissaries and prophets, with Messiah Yeshua Himself being the cornerstone.*
> —Ephesians 2:20

Our outward appearance and behavior may be shaped by the times we are living in, but our hope is anchored to the truth that our inward man has been reshaped and formed by the Father.

Can you identify areas in your life that the Lord has reshaped in a way that only He could?

What areas (maybe anxiety, doubt, fear, direction or another) are you ready to allow the Holy Spirit to reshape or change?

Prayer
Lord, thank You that my hope is anchored to You. Today, I ask that You continue to renew and shape me so I become more of a reflection of Your workmanship – created in Messiah Yeshua for good deeds, which You prepared beforehand so I might walk in them.

Day 3
Fill Me Up Please

Ephesians chapter three has one of the most beautiful illustrations of God's love in the entire Bible. First, I have to preface that statement with the fact that I'm a former supply chain manager who was tasked with scheduling truckloads of food for delivery to restaurants. Space was at a premium, and I was always finding new ways to maximize the space I was given. In his letter to the Ephesians, Paul gives an invitation to pray for the strength to understand the size and depth of the love of Yeshua.

> *I pray that you, being rooted and grounded in love, may have strength to grasp with all the kedoshim [saints or holy ones] what is the width and length and height and depth, and to know the love of Messiah which surpasses knowledge, so you may be filled up with all the fullness of God.*
> —Ephesians 3:17b–19

During challenging times like we find ourselves in right now, the one comfort we can have is that God loves us the same as He did when things were "normal." I know from my shipping days that the capacity of a container is not going to change. I can only fit more of something in by emptying the container of something else.

We learn from Scripture that God's love is vast and limitless:

The width of His forgiveness is "as far as the east is from the west, so far He removed our transgressions from us" (Psalm 103:12).

The length of His sacrifice encompasses the whole world: "He is the atonement for our sins, and not only for our sins but also for the whole world" (1 John 2:2).

The height of His mercy is limitless: "For as high as the heavens are above the earth, so great is His mercy for those who fear Him" (Psalm 103:11).

Simply, the depth of His love can't be contained! "For God so loved the world that He gave His one and only Son, that whoever believes in Him shall not perish but have eternal life" (John 3:16).

Today, we need as much of the Lord's love as possible to strengthen us. His love has no limits, so the question is, how much room have we given Him?

Do you need a refill today of God's love? Write your prayers and thoughts here.

Prayer
Lord, fill me with more of You! Show me things in my life that are taking up too much space, so I can remove them and be filled with more of You.

Day 4
My Words Matter

We all have a comfort zone. When it comes to interacting with people, I think I've been practicing physical distancing my entire life. I prefer a few feet of separation. We are living in a time where a six-foot separation is the standard. Good thing our love for God is not measured by how close we get to each other but rather on how we communicate with one another.

A famous quote from Francis of Assisi says, "Preach the Gospel at all times. When necessary, use words." Whether spoken, texted or posted on social media, right now, words are very necessary. In a time when so many are feeling isolated, we can be the Lord's voice of shalom and hope.

In chapter four of Ephesians, verses 20–29, Paul writes about how, after we receive the truth that is in Yeshua, we are to put off our old self and be renewed in the spirit of our mind. Speak the truth, reconcile with one another quickly, give and not take, share what we have, and build others up according to their need.

During this time, I've given myself a task of going through the contact list on my phone and sending a word of encouragement to people I haven't seen or spoken to in some time – to let them know they are not forgotten and God hasn't changed His mind regarding them. It's been amazing to see the responses from so many who are just happy that someone was thinking about them.

Who can you touch today with a quick note?

Has your mind been renewed by the Holy Spirit? Without words, does your life reflect the fact you are a new creation in Messiah?

If not, read chapter four of Ephesians, and ask the Holy Spirit to renew your mind today. What is the Lord saying to you?

Day 5
A New Day

My home is a little bit busier now. It has become an event center, an office and conference room, a school (high school and college), a playground, movie theatre and so much more. Not that long ago, most of these activities happened somewhere else. Almost every day is starting to look the same, and all the activities are beginning to mix together into a symphony of busyness.

> *Make the most of your time because the days are evil. For this reason, do not be foolish, but understand what the Lord's will is.*
> —Ephesians 5:16–17

But one day still stands out: Shabbat. Shabbat is still a time where we stop and rest in the Lord. The other activities are put on hold, and our "events center" becomes our home again. We can take a deep breath, and remember the Lord's will for our lives. Thankfully – even in this time of uncertainty – we still know exactly, from God's Word, what His will is.

> *Rejoice always, pray constantly, in everything give thanks; for this is God's will for you in Messiah Yeshua.*
> —1 Thessalonians 5:16–18

God's will for us hasn't changed. He is not surprised by the challenges we are facing. His Word is still the same today as it was four months ago. Even if your bedroom has become your office and your living room is now a classroom.

Today, no matter how much it looks like yesterday, find small victories you can rejoice over. List some of the victories you discovered.

Who are some of the people you can pray for today?

Name some things in your life you can be thankful for.

Day 6
Get Dressed, Even If You Have Nowhere to Go

Working from home is one of the biggest changes to my life over the last few months. I've discovered that little things about my "regular" life – things like stopping for my morning coffee, even complaining about traffic, and listening to my favorite morning talk show – bring me joy. Working from home, I don't have those experiences. One thing I don't miss is picking out what I'm going to wear every day. (I'm challenged when it comes to fashion.)

Despite my struggle, and even though I'm working from home, I still get dressed for work every day. The action helps prepare my mind to work, and I'm ready just in case something out of the ordinary happens. In the same sense, I put on the spiritual garments the Lord has provided me each day, no matter what I have planned:

> *Finally, be strong in the Lord and in His mighty power. Put on the full armor of God, so that you are able to stand…*
> —Ephesians 6:10–11a

God has given us instructions – not only to help us right now but to also prepare and help us navigate the challenges that are ahead.

> *Therefore, take up the full armor of God, so that you may be able to resist when the times are evil, and after you have done everything, to stand firm. Stand firm then!*
> —Ephesians 6:13–14a

Read, study, and meditate on God's Word so you can stand firm in times of trouble. Clothe yourself *now* for the battle that is yet to come. You may think you're all dressed up with nowhere to go, but you will be preparing yourself for whatever comes your way tomorrow.

Hope from Ephesians

Do you have a favorite Scripture that you read daily to encourage yourself? Write that Scripture here.

If not, consider reading Ephesians 6:13–18 each day. Journal your thoughts on how this Scripture is impacting you today.

Day 7
Encouragement and Hope

*And pray in the Ruach (Spirit) on every occasion,
with all kinds of prayers and requests.
With this in mind, keep alert with perseverance
and supplication for all the
kedoshim [saints or holy ones].*
—Ephesians 6:18

The apostle Paul wrote four letters, known as the prison epistles, while he was under house arrest in Rome. These letters, three to groups of Believers and one to an individual, contain words of instruction, correction, encouragement and hope. Paul set his mind on building up the followers of Yeshua despite the circumstances he was in. He encouraged them with words of life and reminded them to pray. We all can do the same.

We are blessed to have so many means of communication available to us – phone apps that connect the world, social media, messaging, video conferencing, and yes, we can still send a letter. Let's use this time of separation and isolation to reach out to family, friends, classmates, co-workers and others in our sphere of influence. This is a time of unprecedented opportunity to share the hope that is only found in Jesus to an audience that is listening and ready.

Take a moment to list people in your life that you can encourage today. Send a short message to them so they know you're thinking of them and they are not alone. Begin to pray for them daily.

Hope from Ephesians

For Ezra had prepared his heart to seek the Torah of ADONAI [the Law of the Lord] and to do it, and to teach its statutes and ordinances in Israel.

—Ezra 7:10

Week 9

HOPE
FROM EZRA-NEHEMIAH

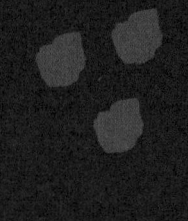

Angela Smith
Executive Assistant

Day 1
In Three-Part Harmony

For thus says ADONAI: "After 70 years for Babylon are complete, I will visit you, and fulfill My good word toward you – to bring you back to this place. For I know the plans that I have in mind for you," declares ADONAI, "plans for shalom and not calamity – to give you a future and a hope."
—Jeremiah 29:10–11

God's plans for His people are often deeper than we know or can figure out. But they are not a mystery to Him. He knows them, and He knows them well.

God gave Jeremiah prophetic words of hope to sustain those of Israel who would go into exile: "...I will visit you, and fulfill my good word toward you – to bring you back to this place" (Jeremiah 29:10). I'm sure these words seemed like a slap in the face at the time. After all, they were in the midst of a war they wouldn't win and were about to be killed or carried off as slaves to a foreign land. Yet, here was God, giving them a hope to hold onto if they would only believe Him. The problem was, the plans He had in mind for them weren't clear to them and didn't make sense in their minds. To them, it was a cacophony of words, jumbled notes, an indistinct melody.

I love to sing. But do you know what I love more than that? Singing in a choir. The layering of voice parts blends together to make such a full and beautiful sound that any music lover would be lifted onto their toes in delight. So rich, full, complete!

Let's take a choir's many parts and break it down into three-part harmony for a minute. For the sake of our exercise, let's use the voice parts of first soprano, second soprano and alto. Typically, the tune for each of these voice parts sounds a little different. Usually the highest voice (first soprano) carries the melody. Theirs is the part of the song that comes out the strongest and most clearly. It's usually the one that captures our attention first and is what we most often try to sing along with. That is because their melody line is memorable.

The second voice part (second soprano) carries a harmony line that is not too far below the first soprano's melody, and it adds another layer and depth to it. This line can be harder to pick out in a song, but it often has just as much melodic movement as the top voice part, and compliments it beautifully.

Then, there's the alto voice part, the third in our example. Uniquely, the alto's part typically doesn't have much movement at all. Most altos go through an entire song sounding out the same notes below the beautiful and flourishing melody line up above, in order to offer a foundation for the song so the other parts can shine. The alto line is not as distinguishable, but like the second soprano, it provides a harmony that complements the melody, adding yet another layer.

Each part is unique. People singing one part don't usually know the other parts; they simply know and sing their own. But when each sings, and their lines combine with the others, what a glorious, sweet sound they make!

When it comes to the story line of the Bible, we hear melodies and harmonies while the voices of the prophets contribute their lines to the song of the ages.

Our God is the Master Composer. The intricacies He has purposefully arranged on His grand scale of time are often indistinguishable to the human ear, unless we strain to hear.

As we journey through the story of Ezra and Nehemiah in the days ahead, listen in for a pattern, a three-part harmony, as God composes another movement in His song through the mouths of His prophets. See if you can make out the sounds of:

1. A melody line, which gives a clear sound of the present and near future
2. A harmony line that rings out future events
3. And yet another harmony line, speaking of a future era when time as we know it will be no more, but we enter the space of eternity

It is in the blend of these voice parts that the sound becomes deeper and more richly layered, having the ability to lift our spirits to glorious heights.

The book of Ezra-Nehemiah (two books in our English Bible/one book in the Hebrew Bible) tells the story of the Jewish people coming out of exile, returning to Jerusalem and rebuilding the Temple and the city's walls. These events were prophesied by Jeremiah and others. This is our melody line. The harmonies underneath it, through the words of the prophets, point us to yet "another day of hope."

> *"For I know the plans that I have in mind for you,"*
> *declares ADONAI, "plans for shalom and not calamity*
> *– to give you a future and a hope."*
> —Jeremiah 29:11

What is the future hope spoken by the prophets? May we keep our ears attuned to the three-part harmony of Heaven, arranged by our Master Composer, in the story of Ezra-Nehemiah.

> *He who has ears to hear, let him hear.*
> —Matthew 11:15

Reflection
Ask the Lord to tune your ears to hear His words and the song of Heaven today, tuning out any distractions that keep you from believing His words about a future and a hope. What is the Lord saying to you?

Day 2
The Stirring Begins

Now in the first year of King Cyrus of Persia, in order to accomplish the word of ADONAI from the mouth of Jeremiah, ADONAI stirred up the spirit of King Cyrus of Persia…
—Ezra 1:1

Ancient Israel had a hope: to return to the Land God had promised to give her. Yet, she had been in exile in Babylon for so long that I'm sure the hope of many began to wane, if not completely disappear. Those who were old enough to have witnessed it told the story to their children and grandchildren. *Family members and friends died in the siege, homes were taken, all of our livelihood was destroyed, we were led away in shame and humiliation, a defeated people, into the land of our captors, and our beloved city Jerusalem still lies in ruins.*

Yet, here they were – in Babylon. They could not just get up and leave. They were being held captive by a force more powerful than they. Even so, by seeking the peace of Babylon, as instructed (Jeremiah 29:7), many had grown accustomed to the new lives they now lived and had forgotten "home."

Many, but not all. An exiled Jewish man in Babylon searches the books of the controversial prophet Jeremiah and uncovers a prophecy: "the number of the years for the fulfilling of the desolation of Jerusalem would be 70 years" (Jeremiah 25:11-14; 29:10,11). After a few quick mental calculations, and realizing that the time is near, Daniel drops to his knees and cries out to the God of his fathers. Fasting and sitting in sackcloth and ashes, he asks forgiveness for himself and his people, who have rebelled and turned away from the Fountain of Living Waters. He acknowledges God's justice and that their punishment is deserved. After confessing Israel's sins and unfaithfulness to the Lord, he proclaims God's faithfulness despite them. And he asks God to hear, forgive, listen and act for His own sake, because of His great compassions and for His city and His own people who are called by His name. Daniel is interrupted mid-sentence as a presence enters his room. A messenger of God, Gabriel, announces that since the moment he began to pray, his prayer was heard (See Daniel 9:1–23).

What follows this prayer? Let's go back to Ezra-Nehemiah where the fulfillment of Jeremiah's prophecy unfolds. God's Spirit stirs the hearts of pagan kings to send His people back to Jerusalem with blessing and abundance (Ezra 1:1). Temple treasures are restored, and men are selected to lead the exiles who desire to go home. Enter Sheshbazzar, Zerubbabel and Jeshua, then Ezra, and later Nehemiah. At the precise time the Lord placed on His calendar, the exiles return in three stages, and three milestones occur: the second Temple is built and dedicated, the people recommit to following the Torah and enter into a covenant with the Lord, and Jerusalem's city walls are repaired.

Can you imagine the initial scene? What would it be like to receive this kind of word from the highest ruler in the country holding you captive: *I've just heard from the God of Israel, and I want you to return to your homeland and worship freely. Here's money to do that. Oh, and here are the plane tickets. What else do you need? It's yours. Go in peace. Your God is the One true God.* Talk about hope fulfilled! No more sheltering in place! Take the journey, cross the borders and enter freely without fear.

Israel's hope was finally being fulfilled and becoming reality! "The Return" had finally begun. But what were the exiles returning to? Could they see beyond the tremendous work that lay before them to the hope of better things than they had in Babylon? After all, life in Babylon had become the new normal. After 50+ years, the second and third generation of Jews born in Babylon could not even imagine what times were like before this. They couldn't relate to the full pain of the exile and captivity as their grandparents and great grandparents could. Jerusalem was not a distant memory for them; it was a memory that didn't exist. They had never been "home," nor did they necessarily long for it.

But for many of the aged and elderly, who waited for God to fulfill the promises spoken through His prophets, the announcement of "the Return" to Jerusalem ignited their hopeful hearts while likely causing concern about how the tired tents of their physical bodies could accomplish such a task. Yet perhaps… just maybe… God would stir the hearts of the younger generation of Babylonian Jews to return home just as He stirred the heart of the pagan King Cyrus to send them home. Thankfully, the Lord God did just that, and "…everyone whose spirit God had stirred up arose to go up to build the House of Adonai in Jerusalem" (Ezra 1:5).

As Isaiah, Jeremiah, Ezekiel and then Daniel all foretold, even after a time of hopelessness and seeming abandonment into the hands of their enemies, the God of their fathers would not abandon the Jewish people, but would make good on His promises. He would restore them to the Land according to His promise to Abraham (Genesis 17:8, 21:12; Jeremiah 29:10,11). God's presence would fill a new Temple (Ezekiel 40-48). God's kingdom would rule over all the Nations (Isaiah 2, Zechariah 8). And, as if that wasn't enough (*dayenu!*), He would send His Messiah, even giving them clues as to who He would be, the exact timing of His coming and His Return (Isaiah 11 and 53; Daniel 9:23-27).

This was a season of expectation, and hopes were high. There had to be a stirring up of these words in their hearts. Perhaps this is the time! Or was this simply one line in the song God was singing over His people? Were the prophets speaking of another time as well, of a New Jerusalem, when our Messiah returns and establishes His kingdom over all the nations of the Earth?

Let's return with them to find out…

Reflection
God alone has the power to stir the hearts of kings and those in authority, and prayer has the power to reveal God's plan to us so that we can partner with Him. (See Daniel 9:23 and Psalm 25:14.)

Do you believe God can stir up the spirit of the leader of your nation to accomplish His word? Why or why not? Today, let's ask the Lord to stir up our faith in prayer for both our leaders and our own expectation that His plans will be accomplished in our world.

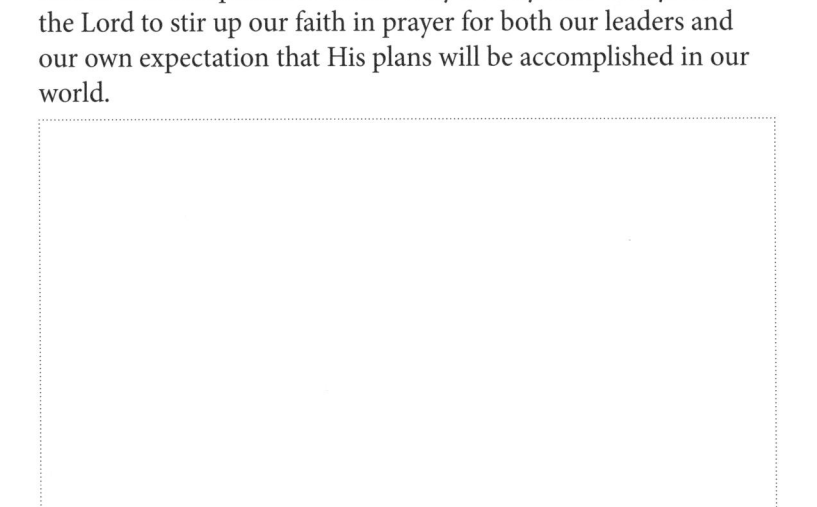

Jerusalem, not Babylon, has always been the promised home of the Jewish people. For all those who trust in Jesus, both Jew and Gentile, we know that one day He will return to make Jerusalem new and establish His forever kingdom. Ask yourself: How might I be caught up in the "new normal" of this world and thus distracted from the hope of my true home, just like ancient Israel was from theirs?

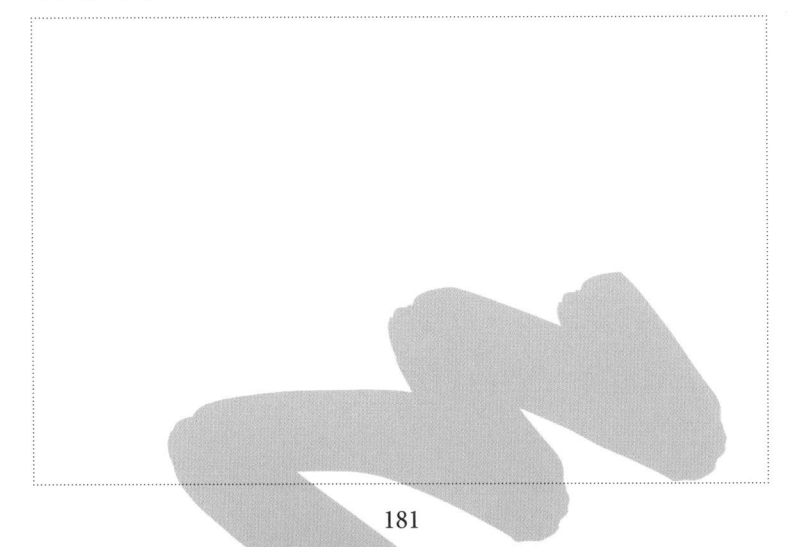

Many Jews in Babylon may have feared leaving their comfortable lifestyles to go to a broken down city and sanctuary to take up the daunting task of rebuilding. Ask the Lord to reveal any fear in your heart about leaving this Earth and its treasures behind for the world to come and the most Treasured One. Ask Him to fill you with hope, joy and peace as you build your life upon the Rock that is unshakeable and eternal. Write your thoughts and prayers here.

Day 3
In the Midst of Opposition

Thus says ADONAI-Tzva'ot [Lord Almighty]: "This people say the time has not come—the time for the House of ADONAI to be rebuilt...". Then Haggai, the messenger of ADONAI, spoke to the people with the message of ADONAI, "I am with you!"—it is a declaration of ADONAI. Then ADONAI stirred the spirit of Zerubbabel son of Shealtiel, governor of Judah, and the spirit of Joshua son of Jehozadak, high priest, and the spirit of all the remnant of the people, and they came and did work on the House of ADONAI-Tzva'ot their God..."
—Haggai 1:2, 13–14

What thoughts must have filled the minds of those who worked to rebuild the former glory of Jerusalem and the sanctuary of God's Glory, the Temple! Stories of how it was before and what it would be like to have God's presence with them again fueled their expectations and motivated their hands to clear away rubble, haul in new stones and cedar from Lebanon, restore the Temple articles for use and prepare to behold the glory of the Holy One of Israel, blessed be He!

Fast forward, and we see the Jewish people committing their lives to follow the Lord and His commandments again, and the walls of Jerusalem, the "City of Gold," being repaired and raised up. The time for fulfillment of God's promises to Israel was finally coming to pass.

Yet, every story of hope has an antagonist or two. When rebuilding our lives on the truth of God's Word, on worship & prayer, and on His sacrificial system (what once was the blood of bulls and goats and now is the blood of Jesus, our Messiah), we will be filled with hope, and we will meet opposition.

Opposition comes in many forms. In Ezra chapter 4, the Jewish people were accused of rebuilding the Temple in order to start a rebellion against Babylon. Their opponents wrote a letter to King Darius, who bought the lie and ordered the work stopped.

The people became discouraged. They shrank back in fear of the King's law, and they gave up. *The time has not come*, they said. Instead, they went to work building houses of their own. Thankfully though, God spoke to His people once again and encouraged them through the prophets Haggai and Zechariah that it was time to rebuild, and that God was with them! Had they so soon forgotten that it was the Lord who stirred up the heart of a King in the first place to do this work, and that this work was truly God's and not their own? Because of their trust in the Lord and the words of His prophets, God stirred them up again to resume the building. He changed the heart of the king, and the Temple was rebuilt!

In Nehemiah 3:33 through the entirety of chapters 4 and then 6, Nehemiah faced insults, threats, intimidation, false prophecies, feigned friendships and the temptation to sin while doing the task God assigned to him. Yet the Lord had promised, "Adonai builds up Jerusalem. He gathers together the exiles of Israel. He heals the brokenhearted and binds up their wounds" (Psalm 147:2–3).

This was a work of Adonai, the Lord, not only a work of Nehemiah's and the Jewish returnees. So, Nehemiah cries out to the Lord, "For they were all trying to intimidate us, thinking, 'Their hands will become weak from the work and it will not be done.' So now, strengthen my hands" (Nehemiah 6:9).

And the Lord God answered his prayer: "So the wall was completed on the twenty-fifth day of the month Elul, in just 52 days. When all our enemies heard, all the surrounding nations were afraid and fell greatly in their own eyes, because they realized that this work had been accomplished by our God" (Nehemiah 6:15,16).

As you read these accounts, can you relate to any of the deterrents sent to distract the returnees from their God given purpose and mission? In these times of struggle and opposition, it is hard to hear the truth of the lyrics of our Master's song. Yet, let the words of the prophets remind you that when the work is initiated by the Lord, it cannot be stopped. Don't give in to discouragement. Let hope arise in your spirit. This underlying part of the song of Ezra-Nehemiah is full of dissonance, but soon it will resolve, and we will hear the beautiful sound of our Master saying,

> *Behold, the dwelling of God is among men, and He shall tabernacle among them. They shall be His people, and God Himself shall be among them and be their God. He shall wipe away every tear from their eyes, and death shall be no more. Nor shall there be mourning or crying or pain any longer, for the former things have passed away.*
> —Revelation 21:3–4

Today, allow God's Holy Spirit to stir you up, as He stirred Zerubbabel, Jeshua, Ezra, Nehemiah and the returnees to dive in, pick up the tools He'd given them, and partner with Him as He fulfills His promises and completes the work He began.

> *Therefore we also, since we are surrounded by so great a cloud of witnesses, let us lay aside every weight, and the sin which so easily ensnares us, and let us run with endurance the race that is set before us, looking unto Jesus, the author and finisher of our faith, who for the joy that was set before Him endured the cross, despising the shame, and has sat down at the right hand of the throne of God.*
> —Hebrews 12:1–2

> *"When people are rebuilding their lives after disaster, hope is often the most important tool in the toolbox."*
> —Mitchel Modine

Reflection

Has discouragement kept you from trusting that God's plans will ultimately come to pass, even if you can't see it now? Perhaps you doubt that a God-ordained relationship will ever be restored or that wayward child will ever return to the Lord. Perhaps a gifting or calling on your life lies dormant now because of the relentless opposition you've faced. Or maybe you tire of believing you will ever be able to return to our first love despite your attempts to do those things you did at first (Revelation 2:4–5). Don't give in to the discouragement of the enemy. His attempts are simply that – attempts. Governments, community and family members along with every kind of resistance were employed against the Jewish people in order, ultimately, to stop God's plans. But we have a sure hope that His plans cannot be stopped. His purposes for Israel and the nations will prevail! Trust Him today and ask Him to turn your discouragement to hope and expectation for the good things He has planned! Share your thoughts here.

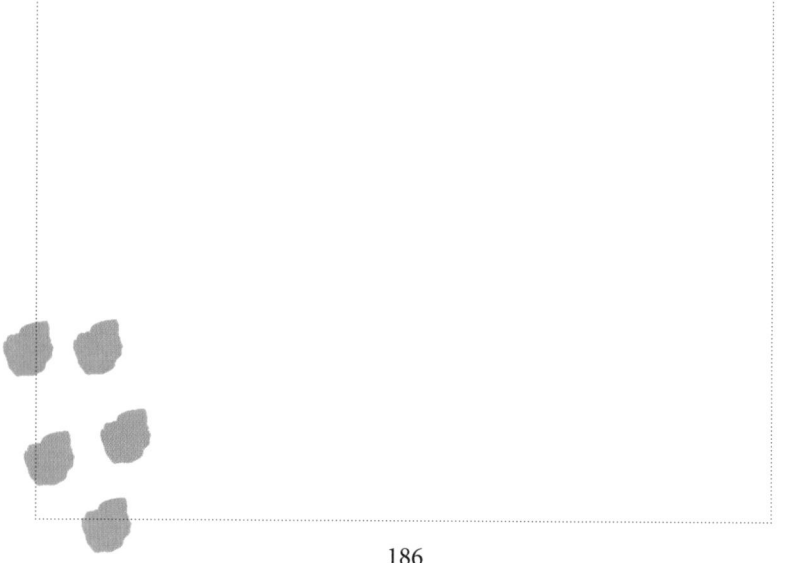

Is there some promise the Lord has given you through His Word that you've stopped believing because of doubt or fear? Are you unsure if you heard Him correctly? Seek Him and wise counsel and then move forward in courage, trusting in the promises of Scripture and in His Spirit to direct your steps along the way.

Day 4
Shavuot, A Musical Interlude

Hope implies an expectation of something good. When you and I hope for something, we have at least a slight expectation that it will happen. When it comes to our faith, hope is the confident expectation that what God has promised will come to pass, and the strength of our hope rests in His faithfulness alone.

There have always been seasons of hope and expectation in the history of Israel, and they have often been sandwiched in the midst of troublesome times. We've seen this in the story of Ezra-Nehemiah, and we see it now.

Right now, we are in a season of expectation, not only in 2020, but right now on the calendar of biblical holidays. This is a time referred to as "the Counting of the Omer." It is the span of days between Passover and Pentecost (or Shavuot in Hebrew) when God reminds His people to count 49 days until the wheat harvest offering, which occurred on the 50th day. On that day, the Jewish people were to bring an offering to the Lord of the first fruits from their harvest (Leviticus 23:15–22). It was a time of waiting and expectation for the harvest yet to come. Tonight, at sunset begins that appointed time on God's calendar, and this should fill our hearts with hope and expectation.

But why? As Believers in Jesus in the 21st century, how can counting up toward a wheat harvest festival hold any significance for us?

Traditionally, Shavuot commemorates the day God gave His teaching, instruction and commandments (The Torah) through Moses to His people Israel (Exodus 19–Leviticus). In unity, the people were gathered together at the base of the mountain when the awesome presence of the Lord descended on Mount Sinai in fire. They were covered in a blanket of smoke as His presence ascended like the smoke of a furnace. The mountain shook as God drew Moses to climb it in order to cut a covenant with His people, setting them apart for Himself as He is set apart. The people waited for Moses to come down from the mountain with God's words for them.

We also remember Shavuot, also called Pentecost, as the day of the outpouring of the Holy Spirit and power upon Jesus' disciples (Acts 2). That, too, was an awesome day. After waiting and counting the Omer, on day 50, the sound of a mighty rushing wind filled the place where they waited with expectation for the "promise of the Father," though they didn't know exactly what to expect. Tongues like fire rested on the heads of those who were gathered in unity. Then, suddenly, new unlearned languages poured forth from their lips as they declared the praises of Adonai to the Jews from many surrounding nations who were gathered in Jerusalem for the pilgrimage Feast of Shavuot. A great harvest followed, though this time, not of wheat, but of people, just as Yeshua had promised.

Those are two examples of significant events that occurred on Shavuot. Perhaps we've just uncovered another melody and harmony line in God's prophetic song. But what about the 3rd voice? Where is the string of notes that rounds out this piece and brings it to its peak, its fulness, a beautiful conclusion?
We are living in unprecedented times, and none of us knows what tomorrow holds. I can hardly keep straight if I'm supposed to stay inside except to go outside, and if I go outside, should I wear a mask and gloves? Yes, a mask, but that will only protect others if I'm sick. And gloves yes, but if I touch something that has COVID on it and then touch something else that someone else will eventually touch they could get sick, won't my efforts have been in vain? Such a *balagan*! (*Balagan* is a Hebrew word for chaos or a state of extreme confusion or disorder.)

And so, how in the world, with all this craziness, are we to be thinking about what God might do on Shavuot this year? Well, it just might be worth our while since we're in a holding pattern of waiting. And, after all, we are called to lay aside the distractions of this world and set our minds on things above where we are truly seated with Him in heavenly places (Luke 8:1, Colossians 3:2–4).

Let's review what we know about significant events in the history of our faith that have occurred on appointed days on God's calendar. The death of Jesus happened on Passover. His resurrection was on Firstfruits. His ascension was during the Counting of the Omer. The outpouring of the Holy Spirit was on Shavuot.

Doesn't it make you curious about what might be in the mind of our awesome God during this season, and, in particular, as we approach Shavuot 2020? Could we be entering the future time spoken of by Paul in Romans 11 when all Israel shall be saved, when the times of the Gentiles is fulfilled and the return of Yeshua is nearer than when we first believed? Yikes –that's a lot to ponder! Still, I'd venture that the Jewish people at the base of Mount Sinai couldn't possibly have pictured what God would do for them on a certain Shavuot in the future (Acts 2). So, is it any wonder why we would have a hard time seeing it now?

As we return to God's story of hope and expectation found in Ezra-Nehemiah, let us listen ever so intently so that we might zoom out from the small brush strokes our Creator has used since the beginning of time to view the broader picture of His story, the full measure of His song. May we glimpse the unbridled object of His affection and the great lengths to which He will go to recapture the love and obedience of the human heart. Who knows, we just might find another reason to have high expectations in this season.

Prayer
Abba, today, please plant in me an expectation for what You plan to do in this season. Please prepare my heart and ready my spirit for this season's harvest and for Your return, revealing to me the role You have for me to play in it.

Reflection

Has your heart become discouraged and your spirit dull as you've waited for the promise of your Father? Ask the Lord to come heal those places of your heart today and give you eyes to see what He sees, the overarching plan of how He is causing all things to work together for the good of those who love Him and are called according to His purpose (Romans 8:28). Write down, for the record, how He encourages you to raise your expectations and set your eyes on Him.

How can you reach out to someone today – a neighbor, stranger, friend or family member – and encourage them to put their trust in the hope of the Scriptures and the Author of their pages? There is no promise God has given to His people Israel and to the nations that has not or will not come to pass. This is good news, and can give others a sure expectation of the future when they put their trust in Him.

Day 5
A Renewed Covenant

Therefore tell them, thus says ADONAI-Tzva'ot, "Return to Me"
—it is a declaration of ADONAI-Tzva'ot—"and I will
return to you," says ADONAI-Tzva'ot.
—Zechariah 1:3

The prophets had spoken to the Jewish people of Judah and now as exiles in Babylon:

- Return to Jerusalem! *Check.*
- Rebuild the Temple! *Check.*
- Return to the Lord! *Check.*

Things are looking good for the Jewish people of the fifth and sixth centuries. Better than they've looked in a long time.

Yet by the time we reach the end of Ezra-Nehemiah, things start to tank. The exiles have returned to Jerusalem, yes, but because of their behavior, Nehemiah fears they will be kicked out once again (Nehemiah 13:18). Though they renewed the covenant to return to the Lord and keep His commandments, observe the Shabbat, not intermarry with those who served other gods and not to neglect the Temple, all their promises come up empty and are broken once again.

Now that's disappointing. This is the place on the page when our hope starts to dwindle. What does this mean regarding the promises of God? Are the words of the prophets powerless? Were they even true? Before we go down that road, remember that the words God gave to His prophets often told about events in the current time, the near future and a time even further in the future. They are always pointing us forward, but what were they pointing us forward to?

Jeremiah gives us a glimpse:

> *"Behold, days are coming" —it is a declaration of Adonai— "when I will make a new covenant with the house of Israel and with the house of Judah— not like the covenant I made with their fathers in the day I took them by the hand to bring them out of the land of Egypt. For they broke My covenant, though I was a husband to them." it is a declaration of Adonai. "But this is the covenant I will make with the house of Israel after those days" —it is a declaration of Adonai— "I will put My Torah within them. Yes, I will write it on their heart. I will be their God and they will be My people. No longer will each teach his neighbor or each his brother, saying: 'Know Adonai,' for they will all know Me, from the least of them to the greatest." it is a declaration of Adonai. "For I will forgive their iniquity, their sin I will remember no more."*
>
> —Jeremiah 31:31–33

A new covenant. Great! They just entered into a new covenant in Nehemiah 10. Yes, well basically they committed again to keeping the covenant God gave them through Moses, which they never had much success keeping. And let's be honest here, neither have we.

So, is Jeremiah talking about "a renewed covenant?" No, God says, a NEW covenant, not like Moses' covenant. A covenant, the terms of which are that God will take their sins and remember them no more and will write His Law on their hearts. Not a covenant where He throws out the Law but now engraves it on their hearts by His Spirit and empowers them to do it. But there is one thing more they need: a *new heart*.

We know that Jeremiah was speaking of the work of Jesus here, right? He was the Messiah, the deliverer who would come and accomplish for His people what they couldn't accomplish for themselves. He would take their hearts of stone and give them a heart of flesh (Ezekiel 36:26). Good, so this is the end of the story, right?

Oh, one more thing: "No longer will each teach his neighbor or each his brother, saying, 'Know Adonai, for they will all know Me, from the least of them to the greatest'" (Jeremiah 31:33).

Hmmm… that doesn't sound like the way things are now, does it? We still have teachers and are still learning from them about who God is, aren't we? Jesus said, "The Holy Spirit will teach you everything and remind you of everything that I said to you" (John 14:26). Still, Paul reminds us that we only know in part (1 Corinthians 13:9). Now. you may ask, *Are you sure Jeremiah 31 wasn't completely fulfilled when Yeshua came?* My friends, don't forget that the story doesn't end with Yeshua's first coming. He is returning to establish His forever kingdom. In Revelation 21:3, John points us to a future time when God is with us as our light. We definitely won't need anyone to teach us then, will we? We will all know Him, for He will be in our midst!

Let's look again. After Yeshua ascended to Heaven (Acts 1:9), what events followed that He foretold (Luke 21:24)? Fast-forward to 70 A.D.: The Temple was destroyed, and the Jewish people were once again exiled, only this time we called it "dispersed." Then what started happening in the 20th century? Jewish people began to return to the Land promised to Abraham after one of the greatest atrocities in human history, the Holocaust. The State of Israel is reborn in 1948 and Jerusalem became the fledgling nation's capital in 1967 (Isaiah 66:8, Ezekiel 37:1–14).

But I thought the words of these prophets were foretelling the return of Jewish exiles from Babylon, you might say Yes, they were. *Were they also speaking of a future exile and return?* Yes. Remember the three-part harmony we talked about in Day One of this devotional series? God's plan is always layers deep; it's a beautiful tapestry of sound, so much deeper than we're discussing even now.

Here is the three-part harmony we're hearing in this section of the Ezra-Nehemiah story:
- Return to the Land

- Return to Me
- I'll return to you

Return to Me, and I'll return to You. The Lord was speaking this to the Jews coming out of exile. He was saying it in 1948, and He is still speaking this to Jewish people today. When will Yeshua return and fill Jerusalem with His glory? In essence, He says, *I will return to Jerusalem, when Israel returns to Me and says, "Blessed is He who comes in the name of the Lord"* (Matthew 23:39).

Reflection

Have you ever thought about Jesus returning to the Earth when the Jewish people return to Him? What does that stir up in you?

Ask the Lord to reveal to you His heart for His people to return to Him. Write your prayer here.

Day 6
A Prepared Heart

For Ezra had prepared his heart to seek the Torah of ADONAI [the Law of the Lord] and to do it, and to teach its statutes and ordinances in Israel.
—Ezra 7:10

Ezra prepared his heart to seek God's Word, to do it and to teach it. Notice what this Scripture *doesn't* say. It doesn't say, "Ezra prepared his heart to be the leader of a great revival." It doesn't say, "Ezra prepared his heart to be well-known and respected enough for kings and people in places of authority to know and call on him for great and noble tasks."

Nope. It only says, "Ezra prepared his heart to seek God's Word, to do it and to teach it."

Observe what else it *doesn't* say:

- Ezra prepared his heart to seek God's gifts or treasures on Earth
- Ezra prepared his heart to seek God's blessings
- Ezra prepared his heart to seek God's favor

Nope. Again, "Ezra prepared his heart to seek God's Word, to do it and to teach it."

The amazing thing about it is that Ezra did, in fact, lead a great revival (see Nehemiah 8-10) and he was called on by a king to take up a great and noble task (Ezra 7:11-28). He was also entrusted with the treasures of God's Temple and received favor and blessing (Ezra 7). But it wasn't because he was seeking any of these things.

As I read this Scripture, I am reminded of Yeshua's words "…seek His kingdom, and these things shall be added to you" (Luke 12:31).

Ezra, as a member of the kohanim (priests), was not even seeking to be established as a priest in Israel. Remember, at this time, there was no Temple. He didn't set his heart on the future of what he could become; he simply did in the present what he knew to do. He sought first God's kingdom, and all these things were added to him.

Why is it important for us to seek to learn God's Word and to do and teach it? It's important because:

- When we seek God's Word, we are seeking Him (John 1:1)
- His Word is exalted even above His name (Psalm 138:2)
- There is great reward in keeping His Word (Psalm 19:10–12)
- It is truth (John 17:17)
- His Word is our comfort in affliction and keeps us alive (Psalm 119:50)
- It keeps our way pure (Psalm 119:9)
- When we seek Him and His kingdom, everything else we need will be added to us (Luke 12:31)
- Those who do God's Word are blessed (Psalm 1:1–3; Luke 11:28)
- Those who do His Word are like those who build their house upon the rock and they will not be shaken (Luke 6:46–48)

Once we learn God's Word, He'll empower us to do His Word. Once we do His Word, we'll be able to teach it, and by the very act of teaching His Word, we'll learn more about it and how to live it. This is a cycle worth repeating.

I must ask myself then, what things am I seeking? Am I seeking to be known or approved by others? Am I seeking to do something great for God or have an abundance of gifts, blessing and favor? Am I seeking earthly treasures instead of heavenly ones? If I answer honestly, the answer is often yes. But it doesn't have to be. In this season, more than ever, in order to have a sure hope, we must seek God's Word. In it is life and all that we need.

Prayer
Lord, I want to prepare my heart to seek Your Word. You said, "Where your treasure is, there will your heart be also" (Luke 12:34). Please help me, by Your Spirit, to clear out of the way anything that is taking a higher place in my life and heart than Your Word. Make learning and doing Your Word my highest goal so that I may be truly blessed and be able to teach others about You.

Reflection
Take inventory of your heart today, and ask God for a heart to seek Him and His Word, to do it and to teach it. You will be blessed and be a blessing.

Day 7
Future Glory

"Who remains among you who saw this House in its former glory? So how do you see it now? Does it not seem as nothing in comparison in your eyes?… The treasures of all the nations will come, and I will fill this House with glory, says ADONAI-Tzva'ot… The glory of this latter House will be greater than the former," says ADONAI-Tzva'ot.
—Haggai 2:3, 7, 9

Life in Jerusalem was being rebuilt after disaster. Expectations were high. In short order, the altar was built, and sacrifices began. It was a time of rejoicing as Israel celebrated Sukkot. Surely, the Jewish hope had not been cut off! Then, after a time, the Foundation of the Temple was laid. The time for fulfillment of God's promises to Israel had finally come!

But then, something strange happened. "But many…who had seen the former House, wept loudly at the sight of the foundation of this House…" (Ezra 3:12). The Lord knew their disappointment and spoke through Haggai, "'Who remains among you who saw this House in its former glory? So how do you see it now? Does it not seem as nothing in comparison in your eyes?" (Haggai 2:3). Yet the Lord assured them, "'I will fill this House with My glory…' says Adonai-Tzva'ot…. 'The glory of this latter House will be greater than the former,' says Adonai-Tzva'ot" (Haggai 2:7, 9).

How could this be? This temple did not at all reflect the beauty and glory of the first Temple of Solomon. But listen for the harmony line of the prophet Haggai in this part of the story. What the people could not see then was the fullness of this promise. The book of Ezra-Nehemiah was not the end of the prophetic story for the Jewish people, but it was one step closer. For, one day in the future, wouldn't One walk through the Temple courts who is the glory of His people Israel (see Luke 2:32)?

And of a time in the future of which John said,

> *I saw no temple in her, for its Temple is ADONAI Elohei-Tzva'ot and the Lamb. And the city has no need for the sun or the moon to shine on it, for the glory of God lights it up, and its lamp is the Lamb. The nations shall walk by its light, and the kings of the Earth bring their glory into it. Its gates shall never be shut by day, for there shall be no night there! And they shall bring into it the glory and honor of the nations.*
> —Revelation 21:22–26

Zechariah told the people in Ezra-Nehemiah's day too: "Thus says Adonai-Tzva'ot, 'In those days it will come to pass that ten men from every language of the nations will grasp the corner of the garment of a Jew saying, "Let us go with you, for we have heard that God is with you"'" (Zechariah 8:23). And again, in Zechariah 14:16: "Then all the survivors from all the nations that attacked Jerusalem will go up from year to year to worship the King, Adonai-Tzva'ot, and to celebrate Sukkot."

Did this happen during Ezra and Nehemiah's lifetime? Not quite. No one but the exiles at that time had access to the Temple or to God's presence. Who celebrated Sukkot during the time of Ezra-Nehemiah? Only the returnees, the Jewish people (Ezra 3:1–4; Nehemiah 6:72b–8:18).

But is that the fulness of what God promised through His prophets, or is there another line in the song that makes up the whole? Jesus, taking from Isaiah's prophecy (Isaiah 56:6–8 – Read this one!), says in Mark 11:17, "Is it not written, 'My house shall be a house of prayer for all the nations'?" Even then, was this expectation met while Yeshua walked the Earth? No, but will He bring His words to pass? You better believe it. It will happen when we all join in the song of Moses and of the Lamb:

Great and wonderful are Your deeds, ADONAI Elohei-Tzva'ot! Just and true are Your ways, O King of the nations! Who shall not fear and glorify Your name, O Lord? For You alone are Holy. All the nations shall come and worship before You, for Your righteous acts have been revealed!

—Revelation 15:3–4

One day, the song God has been composing through the ages will be sung. All the nations will join with the Jewish people to worship the only Most Holy, for His righteous ways will finally be revealed, known and understood. Hallelujah!

Could it be this year? Our hope must be set on the One who made the promises. Though we may not see their fulfillment today, we have hope that the One who promised is faithful, and He will bring His Word to pass. May we wait with expectant hearts for the promise of our Father.

And Lord, haste the day when the faith shall be sight
The clouds be rolled back as a scroll
The trump shall resound, and the Lord shall descend
Even so, it is well with my soul*

Prayer

Lord, prepare me for Your return. Fill me with expectancy and hope. You said, "But understand this, that if the master of the house had known at what hour the thief was coming, he would not have allowed his house to be broken into. You also must be ready, for the Son of Man is coming at an hour you don't expect" (Luke 12:39–40). I don't know where we are in Your story exactly, but I want to be discerning of the signs of the times. May I set my heart on You and Your kingdom, so that I can join in Your forever song!

---

*From the hymn, "It Is Well With My Soul," by Horatio G. Spafford, Public Domain

Reflection
What do we do when what we hoped for doesn't happen in the way we expected it? Did God's promises to us fail? Does the crush of unmet expectations and snuffed out hope mean that God cannot be trusted or that His promises are no longer true? It can be hard to see the hope of the future through the pain of today. It is difficult to imagine something better in the face of a less than hopeful reality. Still, we have the hope of the Scriptures, the promises of the One who never fails. Choose to trust Him today, and look toward the day when your faith will be sight!

ABOUT JEWISH VOICE MINISTRIES

Jewish Voice Ministries International, based in Phoenix, Arizona, is dedicated to proclaiming the Gospel of Yeshua (Jesus) to the Jew first and also to the Nations throughout the world. The Good News is proclaimed through television, media, international festival outreaches and medical clinics/humanitarian aid in some of the poorest places of the world. We plant new and strengthen existing congregations, while nurturing and discipling new Believers. We proclaim the Gospel, the power of God unto salvation. We grow the Messianic Jewish community and engage the Church concerning Israel and the Jewish people. We exist to transform lives and see all Israel saved.

For more infomation, visit:
jewishvoice.org